HEAD OVER HEELS

Jen!
This is the Best
Love story I've
ever read!
Thought you might like
a bit of Lite reading

Love Grinse
xx.

HEAD OVER HEELS

SAM AND JENNY BAILEY

ABC
Books

Published by ABC Books for the
AUSTRALIAN BROADCASTING CORPORATION
GPO Box 9994 Sydney NSW 2001

First published in April 2006
Reprinted April 2006
Reprinted July 2006

ISBN 10 0 7333 1757 X.
ISBN 13 978 0 7333 1757 6.

Cover design by Gayna Murphy, Greendot Design
Cover photograph by Libor Sikora
Typeset in 12 on 18pt Bembo by Kirby Jones
Printed and bound in Australia by Griffin Press

5 4 3

For all those friends and family
who reached out in my time of need and
helped me turn tragedy into something worthwhile.
I couldn't have done it without you all.

CONTENTS

PREFACE

One of the many pleasures of working on *Australian Story* was the opportunity to meet the two young authors of this book. Supported by his family, Sam's brave and positive approach to life, since his terrible accident, is an inspiration indeed. It was a delight to share the story across Australia through our television program and to know that it would offer strength and hope to everyone who saw it.

Goodness knows the portrayal of these qualities is crucial today, when too many of our young Australians are finding their lives difficult to the point of despair. Sam and Jenny Bailey are powerful role models of how to cope when the going gets tough. And who can forget the romance of Sam's surprise on-air marriage proposal to Jenny while she was presenting the ABC breakfast program from Tamworth NSW? It was a magic moment.

Sam and Jenny Bailey have recently received the Rotary District 9650 Vocational Excellence Award, recognising their community leadership.

It's good that Sam and Jenny are invited to travel widely, speaking and meeting audiences personally. Having been part of one such occasion, in Brisbane, I saw how enthusiastically people respond to them.

Their partnership shows what the marriage vows actually mean, "for better, for worse – in sickness and in health", as they meet the exacting daily challenge of living a generous, fruitful life notwithstanding severe physical disability. It's very, very difficult but Sam and Jenny have a depth of character more reminiscent of an earlier generation. And they are one of the funniest and happiest couples I know.

You're in for a rollercoaster ride as you read *Head Over Heels – A story of tragedy, triumph and romance in the Australian bush* and if you respond to the book as I have, it will stay with you as an encouragement on your own journey.

Caroline Jones
Presenter
Australian Story

FOREWORD

Nice. It's such a wimp of a word. It's the gormless word of *Kath and Kim*. It's the faint praise delivered by recipients of unsuitable presents. But inadequate or not, it is the description everyone immediately applies to Sam and Jenny Bailey. It's the word Jenny used in our now famous *Australian Story* episode about meeting and marrying Sam: 'He's the nicest guy I've ever met. I mean why, why would you turn your back on that just because he can't walk and do a few things?' When our producer Caitlin Shea returned from meeting Sam and Jenny, she reported … inevitably, 'They're the nicest people I have ever met.'

What people are struggling to convey about Sam and Jenny Bailey is their warmth, hospitality, humour, sincerity, resilience, self-deprecation and generosity of spirit − an entire bundle of characteristics strongly associated with the bush.

As Executive Producer of *Australian Story*, I rarely meet the people who appear on our program. That's the job of our talented team of producers. But Sam and Jenny became an exception, partly through inclination and partly through circumstance.

I first spotted their story in a magazine in 1999. The article wasn't especially detailed but something about this couple's circumstances and their demeanour in the photographs was very appealing so we decided to check it out. Initially we thought it would be a little 'tail-end' story of about five minutes' duration. But our producer, Caitlin, and our editor, Roger Carter, were so thrilled with the footage and with the personalities of Sam and Jenny that they pressed for a longer story … and the rest, really, is history.

We called the episode on the Baileys 'Something in the Air' and it has remained a firm favourite with all our team – one of those special stories remembered fondly down the years. It resonated strongly with me personally for reasons I couldn't entirely explain. But within three weeks of the episode going to air, the themes hit home in a way I could never have expected.

My brother in the UK was seriously injured in a road accident and just like Sam he was left paralysed. When Sam found out, he called straightaway. One of the first things I did was send a copy of the story to my brother to demonstrate that there would be a future for him, inconceivable as that does seem to people when they first confront what seems unthinkable. In subsequent months, Sam stayed in touch a lot. He even called my brother long-distance and emailed regularly with messages of encouragement. It meant a great deal at a terribly difficult time.

Sam has a rare and indefinable gift for lifting other people's spirits.

And as I now realise, such generosity and thoughtfulness is an especially big effort for someone grappling with the unending problems and complications of life in a wheelchair. The chair is the thing people see, of course. They often imagine that it is the limit of the incapacity when, in fact, the inability to walk is in some ways the least of it.

So, in a number of ways and for several reasons, Sam and Jenny have become special to all of us. They are practically part of the team these days and we do all stay in touch and catch up as regularly as we are able. It's wonderful that they have finally been persuaded to tell their story in this book – because a great deal has happened since that original episode. There is so much that simply cannot be canvassed in half an hour or so of television.

I am sure that as you read, you too will experience a rollicking good time in the company of real friends. Enjoy.

Deb Fleming
Executive Producer
Australian Story

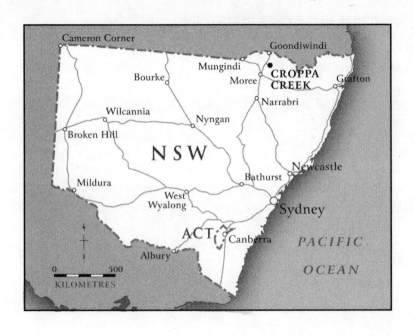

ONE

SIX FOOT TALL AND
BULLET-PROOF

It's amazing how a split second can change your life. Everything is rolling along quite nicely when all of a sudden you experience your very own 'big bang'. Instantly your life is projected into a whole new orbit.

Of course I was oblivious to the significance of events at the time. I was simply minding my own business, having fun on a sunny Sunday afternoon in the Australian outback, when I had what seemed like a minuscule, split-second change of mind. I changed the blinker on my clapped-out old white Kingswood ute from right to left. Just lifted my arm slightly, grabbed the blinker stick on the dusty steering column and pushed it up instead of down. And I changed history. I didn't change the events of the world, but I rocked my own.

In front of me the shiny, melting black tar of the Barkly Highway stretched 647 kilometres from Mount Isa in Queensland to the east

7

and west to Tennant Creek in the Northern Territory. The fumes from my ute drifted back down the dirt entrance to the Australian Agricultural Company's Avon Downs station – near the Queensland/Northern Territory border – where I was employed as a jackaroo.

It had been an unusually quiet weekend at Avon Downs, with most of the station employees away at the Tennant Creek Show. Little more than eighteen months out of school and living on a jackaroo's wages, I was too broke to go to the show, so I had volunteered to stay behind to keep an eye on things and feed animals. But by Sunday afternoon I was looking for a change of pace. I had enough cash to buy a few beers at the Camooweal pub, our closest drinking hole, seventy kilometres to the east, just inside the Queensland border. So I collected fellow jackaroo Johnno and station governess Alex and we crammed onto the sunburnt, vinyl bench seat of my sole possession and headed for town, intent on breaking the boredom. It was Sunday 12 July 1987 – winter, and the middle of the dry season.

There's not much at the Avon Downs station entrance – a sign, cattle grid and a police station, Department of Primary Industries office and a couple of houses down the road a bit. It's in the middle of nowhere, but you're rarely alone. Not for long anyway, because during the dry season the roadway carries thousands of tourists north to the Top End. And playing chicken with the four-wheel drives pulling oversized caravans or precariously top-heavy campervans are hundreds of huge, thundering road trains that carry millions of dollars worth of livestock and general goods to Darwin.

As I went to pull out, one of my mates reminded me that our local buddy and one of Avon Downs' policemen, Peter, had said he'd like to come with us if we decided to go into town. So I turned left instead of right and changed the path of my life forever.

Looking back, there were so many things that could have changed the events that day. When we got to Peter's house, he was having an afternoon nap. Would we wake him or not? We did. Then we faced another dilemma. With Peter joining our adventure, we couldn't all fit into my ute. Instead we had to take Peter's car.

But it was almost out of fuel. He could have offered not to come or we could have abandoned the trip altogether, but we didn't. We were ready to party.

We decided to siphon fuel out of my ute and put it into Peter's car. We eventually found an old bit of garden hose that was perfect for the job. I stuck one end of the hose inside my petrol tank and on the other end, I sucked like hell. I smelled the fuel almost instantly and then a moment later the taste hit my mouth, and spluttering I pushed the end of the hose into an old jerry can. We half-filled the can, and then repeated the exercise to get the contents of the jerry can into Peter's petrol tank.

Finally, we piled into Peter's car – Alex beside him and Johnno and me in the back – and headed east to Camooweal. Already we could taste that ice-cold beer at the end of the road.

We were talking and laughing, telling yarns about the week's events. Then something exploded. The front tyre of Peter's sedan had punctured, releasing thirty-five pounds of air pressure in an instant. Like a fish caught on a hook, the car zigzagged drunkenly down the roadway before skewing left. It leapt the roadside gutter and cartwheeled through the Mitchell grass. All these years later, I can still vividly remember red–brown dust and dirt flying over the windscreen. It was like dancing with a wild dust storm. That's all I saw before being thrown violently out the back window.

I guess in all the excitement it had never entered my head to put on a seatbelt. Having grown up on a property and having worked mainly in the bush, I didn't have that automatic reaction to 'buckle up'. I used to wonder how different my life might have been if I'd click-clacked in the back of Peter's car that day.

At that point, there's a permanent void in my memory. I don't remember being thrown out the window. I don't remember anyone screaming. I don't recall hearing the crunching of the steel car body yielding to the uncompromising hard, dry earth. A few moments I've lost forever. Perhaps I lost consciousness or perhaps my brain chooses to forget. We tend to shut out the worst of it in most events of extreme emotion.

The next thing I do remember is lying on the side of the road. I was oblivious to the vast, blue outback sky stretching 180 degrees above me. Nor did I see the endless plains of the Barkly Tablelands spread hundreds of miles as far as the eye could see. My world had shrunk to a tuft of grass sticking into my ear. The spiky ends were pushing painfully into the soft, suntanned flesh.

That was all I could feel.

I couldn't feel my bruised body lying on the packed earth. I couldn't feel the shirt on my back or the boots on my feet. There was no searing pain from a broken limb, no throbbing cuts or grazes. Nothing.

Then I tried to get up.

I was sending out signals from my brain, but there was no answer. The phone was ringing but no one was home.

A man and woman – tourists I guess – were by my side, speaking to me, giving words of comfort and support, oozing worry and concern. Although I pleaded with them to move the spiky grass indenting my ear, thankfully they didn't touch me. Perhaps they sensed there was something seriously wrong.

Did I panic? Not that I remember. Yet I must have been feeling some trepidation because I remember saying to them, 'Gee, I hope I don't spend the rest of my life in a wheelchair.'

From here on, the memories are confused. I think in any tragedy you tend to lose the sense of time and location. I only have vague recollections of the next three or four hours, during which time medical help arrived from Camooweal. I was stabilised on a spinal board and loaded into the back of a Hilux ute.

I do remember passing the Camooweal pub. There I was, all bound up on a spinal board in the open trayback, yelling at the top of my voice, 'Pull up! Pull up! We'd better have one for the road.' I still haven't had that drink at the Camooweal pub. Maybe I'll go back one day.

Like hundreds of Australians before and since, I have the Royal Flying Doctor Service to thank for a huge part of my journey to hospital. An aircraft was waiting at the bush strip near Camooweal. It flew me, Johnno – who was unconscious – and Alex – who suffered a broken pelvis – to Mount Isa Hospital, where we spent the night. Peter had come out of the accident relatively unscathed.

For me, a few hours down the track things hadn't improved at all. I still didn't have any sensation in the lower part of my body. At Mount Isa Hospital I spent most of the night in x-ray, being photographed from head to toe. The x-rays revealed a dislocated right hip, a broken neck and suspected spinal cord damage. Apart from that, I had hardly a scratch.

My experience at the Mount Isa Hospital is one I'd like to forget. The staff were very impersonal and all the tests left me feeling I'd been stripped bare and placed under spotlights for everyone to prod and poke. I was manhandled from here to there and back again, like a dead carcase at an abattoir. Hardly a word was spoken.

My worst moment came after the tests were finished. As I lay there in shock and confusion, a male nurse shaved the front and sides of my head. He also cut off my jeans and shirt. The whole procedure, no doubt a regular occurrence for him, was done in complete silence. There wasn't one word of explanation, not one word of comfort, not even a greeting. Then a doctor approached and pushed needles into the bald skin above my ears. I felt a sharp sting, instant like a paper wasp, which I later realised must have been a local anaesthetic. Again, no one spoke to me. It was surreal, as though I had the starring role in a black-and-white silent movie.

Next he made incisions behind each of my temples and placed skull tongs on my head. The steel arms rested against each side, over the areas that had been shaved bare. I remember the doctor did say a few words to me, in very limited English; his bedside manner only went as far as suggesting the next procedure 'might hurt a bit'.

He wasn't bloody wrong. Suddenly, I felt an explosion of pain unlike anything I'd experienced in my life before. It was a bit like having a red-hot poker shoved into my brain, turning it to mush. A nail – similar in size to a tack – but sterilised of course, had just been hammered, literally, into my skull. Until then, I hadn't experienced much pain, no doubt because of the spinal cord injury; now I thought I'd gone to hell and back. It felt as if someone had let off a bomb deep inside my head. Then he did the other side. By that time I wanted to slip off the ends of the earth into oblivion. It must take a lot of pain to kill you.

I now know the doctor was putting me in traction, to help keep my spine stable and prevent any further damage. I don't think I could have faced any more at that point. As it turned out, I would be subjected to this procedure twice more over the next week, initially because the tongs had been put on back-to-front at Mount Isa Hospital.

I spent the rest of the night in intensive care. It was one of the longest nights of my life and one of the loneliest. I had spent days living and working in the outback, mustering stock hundreds of miles away from the nearest town or village – never had I felt alone.

Here I was surrounded by nurses, doctors, people who'd chosen to dedicate their life to caring for others and I felt abused and forsaken.

My only visitors that night were Geoff and Carmel Wagstaff, the manager and his wife from Avon Downs. Geoff vividly remembers the doctor who was treating me that night. He asked him how I was, while standing at my bedside, and the doctor told him I was buggered and would never walk again.

'I couldn't believe it,' Geoff said later. 'The doctor should have had more bedside manner and feeling for Sam than to say it like that right there in front of him. He was a real pig. The way he handled it was absolutely terrible.' Luckily, I didn't hear the comment and even if I had, I don't think I would have believed him.

But that nightmare of a night at Mount Isa wasn't over yet. Just when I thought things couldn't get any worse, a nurse came in and told me she needed to put a nasogastric tube up my nose and down into my stomach. She forced the tube inside, its rough edges scratching the tender flesh of my nasal passage as she tried to push it into my oesophagus. I kept gagging on the tube and struggled to escape the pain. By then I was wondering how much more I could take.

Eventually a female doctor came to help. She was like an angel straight from heaven. She held my hand and spoke kindly. Her warm touch and words of comfort helped so much. She was the only medical person who reached out and gave me solace during that first, horrendous night. She explained that I had to have the nasogastric tube inserted because they were flying me to a bigger hospital in Brisbane for more treatment and it was part of the normal preventative measures taken for all spinal-cord-injured patients because their stomach and intestinal muscles stopped working for a period of time. I later found out that a nasogastric tube drains the gastric contents of the stomach, preventing vomiting and nausea, which can be major concerns for someone with an injured spine lying flat on their back and unable to roll over. If I had vomited, the acid could have run into my lungs, giving me pneumonia. The tube was removed as soon as the stomach started working again, rumbling and passing wind. After her encouragement, I tried my best to co-operate and they finally got the tube in place.

It was pretty frightening, at the age of nineteen, to be thrown from the fun and tumble of life as a seemingly invincible, six-foot-tall and bullet-proof jackaroo in the Northern Territory into this nightmare. In less than twenty-four hours, I'd survived a traumatic and violent car accident, been carried on a mad road dash to a waiting Royal Flying Doctor Service aeroplane, had an emergency plane flight and then been subjected to x-rays and painful surgical procedures in a huge, impersonal regional hospital. And all with very little compassion.

During that same twenty-four hours, my parents had been going about business as usual on their busy mixed farming property near Croppa Creek in northwest New South Wales. My mother had just walked into the house on that wintry July afternoon when the phone rang.

A voice said, 'Is that Mrs Bailey?'

'Yes,' replied Mum.

'Mrs Libby Bailey? Do you have a son called Sam?'

'Yes.'

'It's the Sister from Camooweal here.' This was the bush nurse who looked after me before I was flown to Mount Isa. 'I'm afraid he's had a slight car accident.'

It was the phone call all parents dread. But my mother, ever the optimist, recalls that she wasn't terribly alarmed by those words. What she was immediately keen to know was whether I'd suffered head injuries and asked the sister if I was conscious. The sister assured her that I was and that she'd been chatting to me.

'Oh, thank goodness for that,' said Mum.

Then the Sister added, 'But he does have a bit of a sore spine.' This was a huge understatement, but obviously the bush nurse wasn't in a position to tell my parents the full details of my injuries and was trying not to worry them unnecessarily. Another twenty-four hours or more would pass before any of us would know the full extent of the damage. She told my parents to ring Mount Isa Hospital later in the evening to find out more. And so began a night-long phone-side vigil for my parents, who couldn't sleep, couldn't extract information from the detached medical staff and felt completely helpless because I was too far away for them to get to me in a hurry. That night must have been as long for them as it was for me.

Their one point of contact was Geoff Wagstaff. He initially tried to reassure them but eventually, reluctantly, he had to admit that at the moment I had no feeling in my legs.

At one stage Mum said to my twelve-year-old sister, Kate, 'Oh, my God, what if he doesn't ever walk again?'

To which Kate replied, 'Oh, Mum, don't be so stupid. For goodness sake, why do you always think of those things?'

'Well, he's got no feeling in his legs ...'

'Stop jumping to conclusions. He'll be all right. Okay?'

TWO

TAKING THE CAKE

In the early hours of Monday morning, after several attempts, my father managed to speak to a doctor who confirmed that 'at the moment' I had no feeling in my legs, I'd been put in traction and was about to be flown to Brisbane.

We were all feeling optimistic. While I was obviously in shock, I imagined I would be in hospital for only a few days, get better and soon be back on a horse mustering cattle at Avon. Mum, though beginning to panic, still thought something calamitous couldn't possibly happen to one of her children and Dad was focussed on simply doing what had to be done.

I was flown by air ambulance to the spinal injuries unit at Princess Alexandra Hospital in Brisbane. The seeds of doubt were emerging for the first time. Maybe my injuries were a bit more serious than I'd initially thought. I was again accompanied by Johnno on the trip from Mount Isa to Brisbane. He was still unconscious, and the severity of the accident was sinking in.

I arrived at the spinal unit sometime during the night, less than thirty-six hours after the accident. The first thing I noticed was how warm and friendly the staff were. It was such a contrast to my experiences of the night before.

At much the same time, my parents arrived. They had had a day to pack and put everything in order on their property, Bardin, where I'd grown up, leaving my brother and sister with friends. Bill, four years younger than me and in Year 11, and Kate, in her first year of secondary school, were both home from boarding school in Armidale. At that stage, Mum and Dad both thought – like me – I'd be in hospital for a while and then life would return to normal.

Mum and Dad made the five-hour trip through the night, arriving sometime around midnight. As they drove into Brisbane, they saw planes flying into the city's airport and wondered if I was in one of them. But by the time they found their way to the hospital, I'd already arrived.

When they first saw me, they were waiting outside the spinal unit and I was being wheeled from one building to another – bare-chested, my head shaved and with skull tongs inserted above my ears. I must have been quite a sight. But with a continuing sense of optimism, I gave them the thumbs-up sign.

Then I was whisked off for further tests and examinations and my parents were led into a tiny, drab room. Mum has never quite got the image of the curtains out of her head. Large black birds, a bit like ibis, and bright orange flowers on a dull grey background. Strange how your world seems to shrink at a time of intense emotion or trauma and it's the little things that stay with you forever. They probably mirrored her emotions at the time. It must have been a shock for her and Dad, seeing their eldest son lying on a stretcher being wheeled into a spinal unit; their son, who had always dreamt of going home to the family property, who'd revelled in schoolboy sports and always preferred the physical things in life to books and words and computers.

A female orthopaedic surgeon broke the news to Mum and Dad. I guess she knew there was no easy way to tell a young man's parents he would never walk again and she was pretty blunt. There were no pleasantries, no lengthy discussion about the hopes or possibilities, just a couple of simple sentences.

'How much do you know?' she asked them.

'Well, we know that at the moment he has no feeling in his legs.'

'Yes. I'm afraid he's a quadriplegic.'

'What? Do you mean he has no feeling in his body either?'

'That's right,' she said, and paused. 'I'm so sorry.'

Mum said later that it was like having the pillars of Sydney Harbour Bridge falling on top of you. But she didn't cry. My father burst into tears, my mother didn't. It was to be some time before she shed her tears.

Dad says one thing stands out in his memory of that day. 'I vividly remember chatting with the doctor after she'd dropped the bombshell. "What do you do … what line of business are you in?" she asked. I replied, "We're on the land." There was a deadly silence.'

My accident shouldn't really have surprised my parents, however traumatic it was. From a very early age, I was accident-prone. I followed Murphy's Law – if something could go wrong, it did. During my childhood my poor parents spent a lot of their time taking me from our property to the nearest hospital in Warialda, more than sixty kilometres away on a partly gravel road, to be patched up in some way. Let me tell you, it was a well-worn track.

When I was about two I swallowed some of my grandfather's sleeping pills. I came out of his bedroom like a drunken sailor and collapsed onto the floor. At first no one could figure out what was wrong – then someone located the opened bottle. Fortunately we were in town at the time, only a stone's throw from the hospital, so I was in emergency and having the bright red contents of my stomach pumped out in next to no time. When I was three or four, I stuck my finger in a water pressure unit and almost ripped it off. I have a scar down my right leg where they took a skin graft to help save my middle finger. One morning, just before school, I tried to jump a barbed wire fence and miscalculated my leap. That resulted in stitches in two or three different places.

Then there was the time I was run over. I was riding on the tractor with Dad. It was the special treat we kids were allowed when he was driving the tractor in the paddock near the house. This particular day he was working the soil up with a scarifier behind the tractor. After my ride, he sent me off to walk the few hundred metres to the house. He watched my progress and didn't start the engine until I was safely out of sight. Then he put the tractor into gear and started forward. Meanwhile, curious little boy that I was then, I'd spotted something near the wheel of the scarifier and ran back to investigate. The tyre of the scarifier, about twice the size of a car tyre, ran clean over my stomach. My mother will never forget Dad walking across the paddock with a limp little body in his arms. 'I've run over him,' he said with an ashen face. It was a miracle I hadn't suffered life-threatening internal injuries. In fact, I was back home fit and well again after only ten days.

Dad says now, 'From the time Sam could walk he always wanted to be on a tractor, or under a tractor or behind a tractor. We had to watch him because he was always so inclined to be somewhere about when we took off.'

My primary school years were spent at a small bush school at Croppa Creek, fifteen kilometres away. One afternoon, my classmate, neighbour and lifelong friend, Jamie Donaldson, and I decided to ride our pushbikes home. The road was rough gravel and undulating. Part-way home we were pedalling furiously downhill towards a bridge when my front tyre bounced off a rock. The impact sent me flying, arms and legs askew, through the air and when I hit the ground I kept skidding along the loose, coarse roadbase. By the time I'd emerged from the dust I was coated in blood, with a loose piece of skin flapping over my left eye and deep grazes to both elbows and my skinny knees. Jamie was pretty concerned, but I wasn't about to let the adventure end on such an unhappy note, for fear my mother would never let me ride my bike home from school again. So I climbed back on and kept pedalling.

Mum was driving her car along behind us, with my younger brother and sister aboard, after a quick stopover at the small village shop. It took her a while to catch up, but when she did you can imagine the spectacle that greeted her. There I was caked in blood, pedalling like hell and hoping she wouldn't notice a thing. Sadly, she put an end to our pushbike caper then and there, and I was taken to hospital, yet again, to have stitches in my head and knees.

Then there was the close encounter I had with the auger motor. At the time I was still in primary school and helping Dad load wheat out of the grain shed into a semi-trailer, using an auger – a long cylinder containing a mechanism a bit like a flat-bladed corkscrew. The mechanism is turned by a motor, and as it turns it carries the grain along the cylinder, moving it from one place to another. Dad had sent me out of the grain shed to start the motor, which I'd done plenty of times before. It involved winding a starter cord around a pulley and yanking as hard and fast as possible.

I wasn't very big and heavy as a child, and could only just reach the pulley. So when I tugged like hell, the motor unexpectedly backfired, pulling my upper body forward towards the engine. I must have hit the machine with my face because I cut my lip and opened the flesh above my eye. But we were always taught not to give up. So with blood streaming everywhere, I still managed to start the motor before running home to be patched up. Off to hospital we went for more stitches.

I never quite overcame my tendency to be accident-prone. Some years later, I was home on holidays from boarding school and was making a set of shelves in Dad's workshop. I was intent on cutting a piece of pipe with an angle-grinder, when suddenly the power tool flew off the metal and sank its spinning disk into my knee. It was Christmas Eve and we'd had lots of rain. Croppa Creek, which flows through the front of our property, was flooded, blocking the entrance road. So Dad and I headed out through the back paddocks in the four-wheel drive – he busily negotiating the heavy black mud and me sitting beside him with a tightly strapped and padded knee. We slipped and slid mostly sideways for several kilometres but we made it to the hospital and I was stitched up yet again.

It's hardly surprising then, given all my mishaps, that our local GP, Doctor Campbell Wilkinson, was often heard to say, 'Oh no, not Sam Bailey again!'

And all this should prepare you for what my long-suffering mother said when she and Dad arrived at my bedside for the first time. Not 'How are you?' or 'Thank goodness you're okay,' or 'This is awful.' Instead, she gave me a kiss on the forehead and said, 'Well, Sam, you've done some pretty awful things to me in my life but this takes the cake.'

I think I replied, 'You'd better eat your Weetbix, Mum – you might be pushing me around in a wheelchair.' And we were both able to laugh for just a moment because neither of us really believed it could be true.

Nothing could have prepared my parents for the sight of me. When they came to me in the spinal unit, I was lying on my back, my head in traction. My thick dark hair had been shaven off my forehead and sides. There were four holes bored into the side of my head above my ears. Two had been put into my skull in Mount Isa and another two in Brisbane because of the bungle with the skull tongs. A heavy weight, like a brick, was attached to the top of the tongs and suspended over the back of the bed. I had white stockings (known as teds) on my legs up to my thighs which made me look, according to my parents, like a white leghorn chook. I lay there on the white sheets, bare-chested, with just a sheet over my middle. My sunburnt arms, calloused hands and dirty fingernails – the legacy of months working in the Northern Territory – must have seemed strangely out of place in the spotless hospital environment.

My parents were determined to be strong and positive, as they are about most things in life. Mum told me I was going to beat this, there was no way I was not going to walk again, and to ignore what the doctors were telling me. Never for a moment did she let herself think it was a long-term thing. After all, I'd had plenty of accidents before and I'd always bounced back.

THREE

A STROKE OF LUCK

What did I think about my situation in those early few days? I was trying to adjust the image I had of myself. A split second after I woke in the morning, I expected to hear the sound of RM Williams boots creaking across the bare worn floorboards of the jackaroos' quarters, preparing for another day's work on the station.

Dreams in the night were graphic, almost tangible. I'd inhale the salty sweat of my horse and hear the distant bellow of a calf to its mother in the long Mitchell grass. I imagined I could feel the sun's rays absorbing the perspiration from my body as I rode through the dust and flies of a forty-degree day.

But every morning I opened my eyes to a very different world. I'd be staring at the austere ceiling of the hospital room glowing in blue fluorescent light. The imagined smell of salt and sweat would be instantly drowned in that vague clinical blend of hospital-grade disinfectant and sickness.

I'd remember over and over again that I had been in a car accident. Every morning, it would dawn on me that I was actually lying on my back in a spinal unit with a lump of a body that didn't move any more.

I don't remember anyone actually telling me I was a quadriplegic. Perhaps they did and I chose to forget. Looking back, it was probably just as well as my perception at that stage of a quadriplegic was someone who'd lost the use of both arms and legs. If I'd been told in those first few days, 'Sam, you're now a quadriplegic, you'll never walk again, you'll be confined to a wheelchair and life as you've known it will never exist for you again,' it would have been mind-blowing. Instead, I gradually put the pieces of the jigsaw together over a period of time. Like a sponge sitting in egg white, I slowly absorbed the truth.

In that initial week, it was enough just coming to terms with my accident. I was still very much focussed on getting better and returning to my mates and life in the Territory. Then as the week neared its end, I began to suspect that my stay in this hospital was going to be much longer than I'd imagined.

Time passed surprisingly quickly. To start with I was in the acute ward – which is intensive care in the spinal unit – and the lights were on all the time. It was hard to tell if it was day or night and as my body tried to heal, I drifted in and out of sleep. Meanwhile, my whole world existed in a dome-shaped mirror above my head, a bit like the mirrors used at corners where you can't see the traffic. As I lay in traction, I saw everything by reflections in this dome, measuring about sixty centimetres across, or horizontally as I lay on my side.

My parents stayed with me most of the first week, then took a brief visit home to get more clothes and collect my brother and sister, who insisted on coming to see me. Looking back, Kate says, 'I remember walking in and he was lying in the bed and he looked normal, all brown and fit-looking, but his head was shaved and he had these big tongs attached to his head and all this dried blood. I immediately felt sick. I had to go outside because I thought I was going to throw up. I wasn't teary or emotional … being a very naïve twelve-year-old like most country kids, I don't think I fully understood.'

Kate found it shattering to see her childhood hero, her idol, reduced to this. While growing up, she and Bill had constantly fought. He'd often bait her with all sorts of pranks, like bombing her in the swimming pool or teasing her into a race to eat their ice-creams. He'd watch her wolf hers down and then slowly eat his in front of her. I was the one she ran to for help or to deliver retribution to Bill. When she went to boarding school for the first time that year, she'd been desperately homesick. I was the one who spoke to her about her constant, teary phone calls to Mum and Dad, telling her to get her act together, and I often wrote her letters while in the Northern Territory.

Bill and Kate had seen me only a couple of weeks before the accident, when I returned to Armidale for the opening of a building at my old school. Kate has a powerful image of me, as I left her at her school dormitory: 'He signed me back in and I went upstairs and I remember watching him walk across the carpark. I stood at the window and watched him walk all the way across the carpark … it was the last time I saw him walking,' she said.

For Bill, seeing me in the bed in traction was surreal because, to him, I'd grown into a young man in the time I'd been in the

Territory. He saw me lying there, helpless, yet still tanned and muscled, and looking so much older than he remembered.

During that visit, my family stayed overnight with my aunt, Lee McGregor, who lived in Toowong three or four suburbs away. It was approaching the end of the first week since my accident and my mother was feeling the pressure. My aunt drew her attention to the fact that she had her fists permanently clenched. She couldn't sleep at night and refused to take sleeping pills. She had an awful feeling that something else was wrong with me and often at midnight or in the early hours of the morning she'd ask someone to drive her back to the hospital, so she could see me and make sure I was all right. She wonders now whether she actually had a premonition.

However, the pressures of activities at home were mounting and my parents decided they needed to go back to get better organised for the pattern they could see emerging. It was obvious they would be spending a lot of time with me in hospital, but they had a property to run and my younger brother and sister to take care of as well.

I didn't want them to go. I knew they couldn't hang around forever but there was talk of them getting a unit in Brisbane so one or both of them could have periods with me. When they left that morning, Mum was worried. She thought my eyes were wobbly and floating but the staff assured her I was okay. She left for home, reluctantly, an uneasy feeling in the pit of her stomach.

The last family member to see me that day was my aunt, Lee. She recalls that it was after the staff had moved the skull tongs for the third time because they were hurting me every time I chewed or spoke or moved. Lee said I was a completely different person when she visited me that afternoon. Until then I'd been talkative and joking and trying to be as normal as possible.

'When I looked at Sam that day, he wasn't there. That day he just couldn't be Sam. He was obviously unaware of what was happening around him,' said Lee. And it terrified her because she'd seen that look before. She'd lost her husband, forty-four-year-old John McGregor, to a mystery virus only a couple of years earlier. 'I went home and rang Ian [Mum's brother] and told him I was worried. There was something really wrong. Sam's eyes were going back into his eye sockets and he was only semi-conscious. When the nurses came in, I said, 'What's happened?' They said it had been the reaction to the change of tongs …

'Perhaps my vision of what had happened was coloured because I'd seen John in the same situation only two years earlier but I'm also intuitive in lots of ways, and I knew something was wrong, terribly wrong,' said Lee.

Sometime that night I was lying half awake, on my side, still in the acute care section of the spinal unit, facing two empty beds and the nurses' station. Suddenly I felt an overwhelming giddiness, as though I'd had one or two beers too many. My head started spinning and I felt like I was going to pass out. I fought to keep control, fear rising inside me. I thought, 'What's happening to me … what on earth is going on?' But then the feeling subsided and I drifted off.

The nurse in charge of acute that night will never forget what happened. She walked across to my bed, number 37, to wake me and get me ready to be turned onto my back – part of the regular routine of spending four hours on my back, and two on each side in rotation to prevent pressure sores. She couldn't wake me. She yelled out to the other nurse, 'Quick, ring medical emergency … now!'

She drew the curtains around my bed and frantically pressed the foot levers on the big electric bed I was lying in, rotating me onto my back. 'Breathe, you bastard. Breathe!' she yelled at me. All the while, she was pressing her hands to my chest to make sure air was still flowing in and out of my lungs. I noticed her face above me, and wondered what in the hell she was doing. But someone was looking down on me that day and my lungs kept going.

Within seconds the emergency team arrived and took over. I couldn't figure out what they were doing there, why they were all looking at me. After some discussion, they decided to take me for an MRI (Magnetic Resonance Imaging). I was aware of what was happening the whole time, and I remember wondering why all these people were standing around my bed. By then there was no fear or pain or panic. The dizziness disappeared as quickly as it came.

As they wheeled me out of the spinal unit, I was struggling to understand what they were doing. I wondered if they were taking me to the morgue. *Perhaps they think I'm dead.*

By then, Mum and Dad had driven the five hours home, unpacked and started the nightly routine. It was a freezing cold July evening and they'd lit a fire in the sitting room. Mum was trying to cook a hot meal in between phone calls. The phone was ringing non-stop as friends and family discovered they were home and wanted to find out how I was faring.

The phone rang yet again. The voice on the other end of the line was unfamiliar. 'Mrs Bailey … it's Sister Griffith here … from

Princess Alexandra Hospital. I'm afraid Sam's condition has deteriorated markedly and I think you'd better come straight back. Don't waste any time. We're worried he mightn't even last the night. I'm so sorry, I'm so sorry.'

This phone call was far worse than the one from the Sister at Camooweal. Mum put the phone down and screamed out, 'Quickly! We've got to get back!'

That was all Dad needed to hear to spur him into action. Immediately he was in the process of putting out the fire, throwing smouldering logs of wood onto the lawn and dousing them in water. Mum threw the vegetable water onto the smoking remains in the fireplace. She hurled the food into the garden bed outside.

Bill and Kate demanded to be allowed to go to Brisbane. Kate said, 'I didn't want to be bundled off knowing something serious was happening, so we all went.'

The task of driving through the dark for five hours to Brisbane dawned on them: Mum and Dad were exhausted, emotionally and physically. They'd hardly slept all week and had just driven all the way back to Croppa Creek. So they called my uncle, Ian McGregor, in Warialda. He dropped everything and arrived at Bardin an hour later. The five of them set off about 9pm with Ian at the wheel – and facing the very real prospect that I mightn't be alive when they arrived.

They walked into the intensive care unit at about 2am to find me barely conscious, attached to tubes and monitors, with a ventilator in my mouth to help me breathe. My mouth was red raw and bleeding. I can't imagine what a shock seeing me must have been – but at least I was alive.

When I regained consciousness, I realised that I had been moved from the acute ward in the spinal unit to the intensive care unit of the hospital. Mum and Dad were at my side and I tried to talk, and couldn't understand why I couldn't. It was a strange experience, like being inside a bubble. I could see and hear everything around me, but I couldn't get through to them.

Later I found out I'd suffered an ischaemic episode (inadequate supply of blood) to the cerebellum, or pons — the area of the brain which controls co-ordination, including eye control, swallow and motor co-ordination — due to damage of the vertebral artery. In layman's terms I'd suffered a stroke, and scans showed that while I'd only suffered one episode, it affected two areas of my brain. I lost the ability to move my eyes to the sides and they were no longer parallel. I'd also completely lost the use of my already partly debilitated left arm.

But my parents weren't giving up on me. They were worried that if they all arrived together in the middle of the night, I might panic and think there was something seriously wrong. So they came one or two at a time, trying to be bright, telling me what was happening at Bardin but not knowing whether I was absorbing the information.

To make way for the constant stream of medical staff monitoring me, it was decided that Mum, Dad and Kate would spend the remaining few hours of the night at the Red Cross emergency accommodation in the hospital grounds, while Ian and Bill went to stay with Lee at Toowong. For Mum, Dad and Kate, the warm welcome and the piping hot cup of tea from the wonderful Red Cross volunteers more than made up for the unusual experience of bedding down on the floor side-by-side with a group of strangers.

But everyone there had a common bond and every time the phone rang, each person froze and waited to see who would be summoned. Fortunately it was never Mum and Dad.

Next day I was still in grave danger and my family took turns to be at my bedside. Bill sat there for hours. My sixteen-year-old brother was the practical joker of the family and sporting hero at boarding school and I couldn't even ask him how his footy was going. Mum, Dad and Kate came and went. When they weren't sitting with me they paced the hospital grounds or sat in the little open-air cafeteria, playing with mugs of tasteless coffee. No one felt like eating. There was a chapel in the grounds but Mum felt she couldn't go running in asking God for help when she hadn't really paid Him much attention during the past few years.

That day the doctors explained to my parents what had happened and recommended using an anticoagulant. They said the best treatment was soluble aspirin. If that didn't work then I wasn't expected to last another night. They were also worried that I'd lost the ability to gag and swallow – which meant I'd need to be fed by tubes – and thought I may have suffered some brain damage. If I survived, I was likely to be a vegetable – no legs or trunk, only one arm, brain damage and unable to swallow or feed myself. Not exactly what Mum and Dad wanted to hear, but they weren't giving up.

That evening Dad came to say goodnight – on his own. Much later, I found out why. My doctor from the spinal unit, Dr Bill Davies, had called my parents into his office. 'Sam's not out of the woods yet by any means, he'd said. 'The next few hours will be crucial. I think you should both go in and say goodnight, just in case …'

For the first time, Mum's courage failed her. 'I can't say goodbye,' she told Dad. 'There's no way I'm kissing him goodbye.' In fact, she couldn't even go back into my room. She said later, 'I couldn't walk in there thinking this was the last time I was seeing him, which seemed extraordinary when we'd been with him virtually day in, day out until that point.'

It was Dad who found the strength on that occasion. When he walked out of the emergency room after saying goodnight to me, he told Mum, 'He's really peaceful ... he looks all right. Don't worry. He'll still be there in the morning.'

Why had he felt so confident I'd make it through that night, I asked him later. He said he walked into the room and told me, 'Righto, Sam, it's time to go. I'll say goodnight ...' And this little weak hand came out from under the sheet and gave the thumbs-up sign. 'I knew then you'd be all right.'

I was lucky. In their different ways and at varying times throughout my ordeal, my parents both gave me the courage and strength that I needed to get through. Mum says, 'Whenever I couldn't cope with something, Graham always had enormous strength ... it's been like that all the way through our marriage.'

Dad explained to me that he was absolutely devastated when I had my accident but he felt he shouldn't show it because that wouldn't have helped me. 'I suddenly realised that his life was destroyed, in a sense, at that early stage and I thought, "I can't fall in a heap. I've got to wear it as best I can." I had to put the anger and frustration out of my mind. I couldn't cope with the problem – help Sam and look after Kate and Bill as well, they had to share the problem too – if I fell in a hole.'

Dad took the attitude, 'I had to say, "Well it's happened, I just have to get on with it" – as Sam was. He wasn't falling in a heap and he was the one with the problem, so he inspired us to cope.'

I guess in a way we all took strength and inspiration from each other and that's how we got through.

Perhaps a miracle happened that night because I was still there in the morning. Dad had been right. But Mum was worried that she couldn't communicate with me and was determined to find out if I had in fact suffered brain damage. She noticed that I could blink. It gave her an idea. She told me she would ask me some questions and I was to blink for the right answer.

'Am I the Queen?'

I did nothing.

'Am I the Pope?'

I did nothing.

'Am I your mother?'

I blinked.

'Am I wearing a green shirt?'

Nothing.

'Am I wearing a spotty shirt?'

I didn't respond.

'Am I wearing a striped shirt?'

Again I blinked.

Mum was elated. She knew, perhaps as only a mother could, that my brain was okay.

After lying in a bed constantly, with my head on a pillow, the back of my head was driving me insane with itchiness. You can imagine how frustrating it was, unable to communicate and unable to scratch my head. Mum sensed something was wrong

35

and asked whether my head was itchy. I blinked and she scratched my head. She then disappeared and returned with a bottle of baby oil, which she rubbed into the back of my head. It was heaven, absolute pure bliss.

The following morning they were all back. It was heartbreaking for them visiting me that day, partly because my mouth around the ventilator looked so red and sore. The ventilator was needed straight after my attack – I'd lost seventy-five per cent of my lung capacity through my spinal injury and the strokes made it even more difficult to breathe. But two days on, I was in absolute bloody agony. Somehow I managed to raise my arm a bit and point towards my mouth. Mum finally got the message but when she asked the nurses and a young doctor to take out the tube, they said they'd have to speak to the senior doctor in charge.

Nothing happened. My mother asked again … and again. Still she was told, yes, they would do something but twenty-four hours later they hadn't. I was getting to the end of my tether and repeatedly pointing, pleading with my parents to get something done. The young doctor on duty promised, 'Yes, we'll take it out soon. We'll definitely take it out this afternoon.'

Mum and Dad returned later that day. Still I lay there red raw and aching, ventilator firmly in place. It was too much for Mum, who screamed, 'If someone doesn't come and take this thing out of his mouth, I'll pull all her tubes out!' – indicating to the unfortunate young woman in the next bed, who had received a kidney transplant.

She wouldn't have done it, I'm sure, but no doubt the poor woman had a few anxious moments – and the gobsmacked nursing staff certainly took Mum seriously. The startled young doctor on duty assured her the ventilator would definitely be out by morning. When Mum arrived next morning, the staff were in the process of removing it from my mouth. She suspects they saw her coming. She might have been right.

By now, Mum and Dad had reached what was for them the lowest point in my entire journey as a quadriplegic.

On one occasion, as they were returning to the spinal unit, they came face to face with George Browning, the Bishop of Brisbane, whose son Richard had been at boarding school with me at The Armidale School (TAS). He was dressed in his ceremonial purple vest, white collar and the chains of his office, along with his suit. He was obviously going in the same direction and Mum panicked.

'You're not going to see Sam?'

'Yes.'

'Oh, please don't. If he sees you leaning over him with all those chains, he'll think he's doomed. He mustn't know he's so sick. He mustn't know.'

Bishop Browning was stunned. He didn't quite know what to say. 'Libby ... I must admit, I've never thought of it that way.'

'I'm sorry, it's not that I don't appreciate you coming, but I just don't want Sam to think there's something wrong. I'd love you to come again ... but later on, when he's okay,' said Mum.

Bishop Browning didn't come and visit me that day. He came back a week or so later, and when he did he told Mum, 'Libby, that was a great lesson to me. It never occurred to me that my visit might be interpreted that way.' Down the track, we all laughed about it a lot. It must have been quite a spectacle, my mother telling the bishop not to dare go near her son because I might think he was delivering my last rites.

Bishop Browning's son, Richard, who became a regular visitor, was with his father that day. He told me they left – having not seen me, of course – deeply concerned for my wellbeing, but with little doubt about where my determination and directness of speech came from!

Occasionally, events in our lives are unexplainable. Unknown to me, the boys at TAS were quite affected by news of my accident. My former house master, Jim (Jungle) Graham, later told me, 'The effect of your accident was most obvious in Tyrell House [the boarding house in which I had been house captain two years earlier]. The boys talked about it and wanted to send a card and all that sort of thing. After a couple of days in discussion, a couple of them suggested – because we knew things were pretty desperate – they wanted to have a chapel service.'

The service was arranged for Tyrell House boarders and anyone else who wanted to come. It took place one night after the evening meal. Jungle takes up the story: 'The boys wanted to manage it, and the chaplain was involved. One of the boys who wasn't a good organist wanted to play the organ, so obviously he did. It was strange. There was a great depression, which was almost tangible, a collective depression that seemed to go through all the boys. The fact the boy who played the organ played badly was almost symbolic of the general feeling, which is a very strange thing to say.

'The boys were very focussed. It seemed to be an expression of how serious it all was. Now I don't know if some of the lights in the chapel were not working or if the electricity wasn't up to its normal power, but the chapel seemed darker than usual. It was most extraordinary. Everything was subdued. The chapel seemed darker, there was this very heavy feeling of worry and concern and they all seemed to mix together.'

After talking to my mother, Jungle discovered the service took place on the same night I suffered my stroke and my life hung in the balance.

I spent twelve days in the intensive care unit, or ICU. During that time a doctor performed a tracheotomy – surgically inserting a tube into my trachea – to prevent everything in my mouth flowing into my lungs. It was necessary because I'd lost the ability to swallow. Gradually my health improved.

The doctors often brought young trainees into the ICU as part of their medical education, and from time to time I was aware of a circle of people around my bed. The doctors would tell them what had happened to me, an impersonal account that made me feel like a specimen under a microscope.

When I popped into the ICU months later, the head of the unit was amazed to see that I could point out where I'd been. He couldn't believe I had been conscious the whole time. I reminded him he needed to be careful in situations like mine. Some of the comments made around my bed might have had a huge negative effect on how I coped. They assumed I had been totally away with the pixies and oblivious to everything that was happening. They couldn't have been more wrong.

Two weeks after I'd been rushed to the ICU, on the verge of death, I clawed my way back to the spinal unit to start the long road back to the real world. When I left intensive care, I still hadn't regained control of my eyes or my left arm and everyone, except my mother, was probably wondering if I'd suffered brain damage. But I remember it all; the whole experience is as clear as a bell.

FOUR

THE SIMPLE THINGS

I was nineteen years old, on the brink of adulthood and independence. Suddenly I didn't know how to feed myself, go to the loo or brush my teeth. I couldn't sit up in bed by myself or dress myself and certainly didn't know how to get into a wheelchair.

Picking up a pin with my fingers was beyond my wildest imaginings. It was the most impossible task in the world. It was like asking someone who was afraid of heights to fly to the moon.

As for walking, that word was now permanently erased from my own private dictionary along with running, rugby, horseriding, surfing and quite a few others.

The only comforting thought was that I knew I wasn't alone. I'd joined an exclusive club of 10,000 to 12,000 spinal cord injury sufferers in Australia. Between 300 and 400 new recruits join the club each year – that's about fifteen for every million of our population. At the Princess Alexandra Hospital I was surrounded by about forty new members. I had a better chance of joining the club than most. This club has a preference for males in the eighteen to twenty-five age group involved in motor vehicle accidents. Each year the Australian Institute of Health and Welfare National Injury Surveillance Unit at Flinders University in South Australia prepares a report on Spinal Cord Injury (SCI) in Australia. It reveals that a fifth of SCI sufferers are typically between eighteen and twenty-five years of age, nearly 80 per cent are male and one in five has been a passenger or driver in motor vehicles involved in accidents.

I injured my spine in the cervical segment of my vertebrae, in my neck, as opposed to the thoracic (the rib area) or lumbar region (lower back). Around 150 Australians suffer a similar level of spinal cord injury each year – more than half of all injuries. I can't pick up a pin because I'm a quadriplegic or tetraplegic at level C7 on my right side, C6 on my left. My brain sends messages, like a telephone call, but there's no reply from my chest down. If the message is for the muscles in the top of my arms something picks up the receiver, but below that it just rings out. So when I tell my hands to use the fine motor skills required to pick up something as small as a pin, the muscles don't pick up the handpiece.

I didn't bruise my spinal cord. I didn't even crush it. If I had, I might have been what is called an incomplete quadriplegic – someone who can maybe walk a little, but who has no feeling below the injury and some loss of function. What I had is called a complete lesion. I cut my spinal cord virtually all the way through. I did a bloody good job and there's no sewing it back. Maybe one day they'll find a cure but for now, the phone has been well and truly disconnected. I'm what is called a complete quadriplegic.

In the beginning I thought I'd only have to take 'walking' and 'mobility' out of that personal dictionary I was telling you about. But I was wrong. I also had to cross out words like 'sweating' and 'shivering'. I had no temperature control. Not only did my body not feel touch, it also didn't feel hot or cold.

I'll never forget my first shower. The nurse wheeled me into the bathroom in a special shower bed and lined it up near the shower rose. I heard her turn on the tap and could hear the water running and pouring down the drain. I lay there waiting for her to start washing me. The time passed and nothing was happening.

'Are you going to give me a shower?' I asked.

'I'm halfway through,' she replied.

I couldn't believe it. She'd started at my feet and I hadn't felt a thing.

The first time I bathed myself I watched the water hitting my body, cascading down my skin. I was all shiny and glowing with the droplets and the dark hair on my bare chest and legs lay flat under the flowing water. I'd discovered another word to cross out of my dictionary. 'Wet.' I didn't feel wet.

Then there was the matter of my bladder and bowels. When I was in the acute unit before my stroke, the thought came into my head that I hadn't done a pee for three or four days. I thought I'd be all wet. I put my hand down to feel my crutch and touched a tube coming out of my old fella. The nurses had been emptying my bladder with an indwelling catheter the whole time, and I hadn't even known. I also hadn't emptied my bowels for days, and eventually I asked a nurse about it. It felt so embarrassing to be a young man entering adulthood and having to ask a female a question like that. She was unfazed, telling me, 'Oh, that's all taken care of at night time and you wouldn't even know.' They had been using suppositories to empty my bowels. Boy, did I have a lot to learn.

So there I was – schoolboy rugby representative and keen athlete, fencer, jackaroo, steer rider, aspiring farmer and all-round country bloke – literally without a leg to stand on, and dealing with a few other challenges as well.

I'd hit rock bottom. A month after my accident, I was facing the toughest time I'd been through so far.

With hindsight, I suppose I was going through the grieving period. I guess I experienced all the normal stages – sadness, anger and denial. I don't really remember the anger so much, but there was denial. I kept hoping I'd wake up and find out it was all a bad dream, a rotten nightmare. But each time, when I opened my eyes, nothing had changed.

We've all experienced waking up in the night in a lather of sweat after a bad dream. When you open your eyes, you think, 'Thank God that wasn't true.' But for me, the dreams were true. Some nights it happened over and over. The awakenings were such a let-down because the result was a shock, again and again. I would quickly close my eyes, trying to shut out the awful reality, willing myself back to sleep – back into oblivion. It was like floating at the bottom of a swimming pool, in the dead leaves and murky, lifeless water. I could have stayed down there, lonely and sad, surrounded by plankton, drowned bugs and grit.

It's a pretty simple choice really. There are only two options – sink or swim. I couldn't see much life down there at the bottom so I decided to swim.

I had plenty of reasons to swim. I only had to look around me at other patients in the spinal unit who were worse off than I was. In the bed next to me was a guy called Gary. He was completely paralysed from the neck down and needed a respirator to breathe. When I was having a bad day, struggling to sit up in bed or to transfer into my chair without landing in a crumpled heap on the floor, I'd see him waiting for the nurses to help him sit up, to dress him and get him into a chair. I guess that was always in my face and so, as hard and bloody tough as it was, there was always someone else doing it a lot bloody tougher. That stopped me throwing the towel in. I used to think to myself, 'You could be like that.'

Another fellow patient was a guy whose injury was a fraction higher than mine, who had been there for a couple of months before I arrived. He used to come up every now and then and we'd chat about the steps towards going home. He'd been through the worst of it and let me know things would get better.

In fact, there was a great bunch of patients in the unit when I was there. There are probably good and bad batches. I had a cracker bunch. Mainly young males, in their late teens or early twenties. They had suffered diving injuries, motor vehicle accidents and in one or two cases, freak accidents such as falling through the ceiling of a house. In that environment I felt safe and secure and there was a camaraderie between us because we all had the same problems. There was a lot of joking and carrying on about our different disabilities. And because we weren't there for only a day or two – some people end up in spinal units for twelve months or more – it was almost like a family.

Then there were my own family and friends. I was swamped with cards, flowers, phone calls, letters and fruit. My room looked like a florist's shop. At one stage we had to distribute some of the flowers throughout the other rooms in the spinal unit. Ten to a dozen letters turned up every day. The nurses had never seen anything like it.

One family friend wasn't surprised by the response. She wrote, 'I know you didn't set out to test the efficiency of the grapevine and bush telegraph, but you must realise by now that news of your accident reached every nook and cranny of at least three Australian states in under twenty-four hours – surely an all-time record!' Another wrote, with typical dry Aussie humour, 'I hear via the grapevine Sam that last week wasn't crash hot for you!'

The humour continued: 'I hope they're looking after you all right up there – good food and nurses with the TV in the right position … I suppose you won't have even seen a TV for a while, just fences, a few Brahmans, bit of Mitchell grass and of course, the odd Bundy!'

Then there were the words of encouragement, '… you've got some bloody good friends here [at Avon Downs] who are going to stick by you through thick and thin.'

And: 'There aren't many people I know that have what it takes to make a go of any situation they may find themselves in. But you mate are one of the lucky few …'

Another writer said, 'Remember – you're "Territory Tough" now, so keep striving.'

And: 'Look mate, I'm not very good at this but I think you know what I'm trying to say and how I'm feeling for you, it's not "Poor Sam", it's "Come on, Sam"!'

Some of my friends found it hard to know what to say, but said it anyway. Like the mate who wrote, 'It's taken me a while to sit down and write to you, mainly cause I didn't know what to say – then, I suddenly thought Sam wouldn't mind what I wrote as long as it isn't "wimpy" – right?' Another said, 'For a couple of weeks now I've been wondering how to start this letter and I still don't know. I'm really sorry, mate!'

Then there were words of wisdom. 'I guess the only thing you'll never be able to do is play rugby … you gave it the best years of your youth and made all the friends and that's what it is all about anyhow, Sam – friendship.' And: 'There is little doubt that you are going to get as much out of life as you would have before the accident, it will of course come in different ways, but it is almost inevitable that you will give even more to life, simply through your determination to conquer every obstacle.'

I hope I haven't failed them, all those people who wrote to me or phoned me or sent me flowers or bowls of fruit. They certainly inspired me to keep going.

The person who was there for me the most, apart from my immediate family, was my girlfriend at the time, Kim McConville. During the five months I was in the unit, she visited every weekend except two. That was a huge commitment when she was studying at university more than five hours' drive away. Sadly Kim's and my relationship ended a few months later, unable to withstand the pressures and guilt I felt after my accident. But during my time in the spinal unit she came, weekend after weekend, with conversation and support, love and cheerfulness.

Her visits helped take the pressure off Mum and Dad because they couldn't be there all the time, much as they would have like to be. They visited every ten days or so in that initial period, but they had the farm and two other kids to support, so they came less often as I began to improve.

There were lots of other visitors as well, including my aunt, Lee, and my godmother, Annie Ross, who also lived in Brisbane. During those first eight weeks when I was on my back and struggling to feed myself, they made up a roster between them to help. The nurses were there but Lee and Annie felt this was something they could do to make a difference.

One of the most overwhelming displays of support came about a month after my accident when six of the jackaroos and the stock camp cook, Sandy, came all the way from Avon Downs to visit me. It took them twenty-six hours to get to Brisbane by bus from Mount Isa – after a three-hour drive by car from the station – a trip which was funded by the Australian Agricultural Company. They arrived three days after I got out of the ICU, when life was looking pretty ordinary. They couldn't have timed it better.

I think my appearance was quite a shock to them. The Sam they knew was six foot tall, tanned and generally pulling pranks on them in the stock camp. While they'd obviously been kept up to date with my progress, like me they were pretty naïve about what being a quadriplegic actually meant. They walked into the spinal unit and saw me lying there, with the skull tongs in my head, unable to move, by now reduced to skin and bone and my tan faded away.

One of those jackaroos, John Ryan, recalls, 'We didn't know what to expect and when we first walked in and saw all these things hanging off his head we were so shocked … it didn't look like Sam. He looked like someone we didn't know … it blew us all out of the water when we saw him in the flesh. That's when it really hurt everyone.' As hard as it was for them, they all came to visit me four days in a row, as well as spending time with the other back-seat passenger in the accident, Johnno, who had been released from hospital by then. He went on to make a full recovery. They also brought good news about Alex, whose broken pelvis had mended in a month, and she was back at Avon.

They visited me in pairs, so they wouldn't wear me out. We laughed about the fun we'd had in the stock camps, telling jokes, reminiscing and talking about the latest news from the Northern Territory. At times I couldn't help drifting off, I was still so weak, but I wouldn't have missed them for anything.

Despite my dramatically changed appearance, John said, 'Sam's voice still reverberated around the room like it always had. And he made us all feel comfortable. Just like he did at the stock camp, he involved everybody and had a special little comment, a joke for each person. He made it so much easier for all of us.

'We were telling him what we were doing on the station, but it was hard when I realised he was never going to do it again. So then, we tried to reminiscence rather than talk about the future …'

John kept a diary and on Wednesday 13 August, the day they returned home to Avon, he wrote, 'Hope it doesn't send him backwards'. They all felt their visit had cheered me up, John told me, and I was back to my usual jovial self by the time they left. It was true, their visit really lifted my spirits, and I felt sad when they left. I would have done anything to be going with them.

But I gather the trip home was a very long, quiet, sombre one. While they'd been warned it wouldn't be easy visiting me in hospital, it had been much harder than they imagined. 'We were still talking about that for a long time in the stock camp. It was a trip we were glad we did, but it had a profound impact on us all,' John said. Apparently it was to be quite a few weeks before the normal fun and laugher returned to the stock camp.

Another visitor I've already mentioned was Richard Browning. He began to come regularly, often with a carload of friends from university. They would arrive en masse – loud, noisy, boisterous, full of one-liners. Their visits were like one long stand-up comedy routine without the audience. Jokes bounced all over the place and we laughed ourselves sore. The visits grew into major events, almost parties, and everyone was included. They enveloped staff and other patients in the spinal unit. In fact, everyone at some time was touched by their visits.

Richard, who is now an ordained Anglican minister and works in an Anglican school in Canberra, says the visits helped him at a time when he was wrestling with issues about his own life, faith and purpose. He told me, 'In you, Sam, I had the avenue to face the reality of a life under a very real threat … meeting with you clearly gave me something. It would have something to do with your enthusiasm for the life we have, regardless of where we find ourselves. It would have something to do with my own faith. Can I join another at the edge of an abyss and have something to offer, even if it be simply my presence?'

While I felt buoyed by Richard and his friends' visits, it was mutual. And don't worry, I gave as much as I got. Richard and most of his friends who visited were physiotherapy students. They had been learning that one of the side effects of spinal cord injury, when the injury was above a certain level, was a full erection, sometimes for days and days. And it is true that during some of those earlier visits, there were days when the marquee stood impressively erected. My visitors would wait until there were nurses around, the younger and prettier the better, and the comments would start flying. 'Nurse, I think Sam is a bit faint. Are you sure he doesn't need an infusion to keep flying that flag?' 'Nurse, what are you doing to the man? Be professional, please. He can't help it. It's not Sam's fault. What are you doing?' 'Hey, Sam, you don't know this, but it looks like you are so keen to walk out of here you are growing another leg … and the nurse isn't quite sure whether to fit a shoe or get out the nail polish.'

One particularly pretty nurse actually left. She walked out of the room! We thought for a moment we'd offended her, but she came back, having recomposed herself enough to complete her work fixing up my teds (the long white stockings) and straighten me in bed.

My visitors' antics were never crude or mocking. They took on the role of speaking about the bleeding obvious, helping everyone laugh. Looking back, it probably helped me through the grieving process, allowing me to release the trauma bit by bit as I faced my future.

Day in, day out, my greatest personal help came from the nurses, my doctor, occupational therapist and physiotherapist. Again I was lucky. I happened to get the head occupational therapist and the physiotherapist-in-charge. They were the best the spinal unit had to offer and I believe I owe them a lot.

For the first couple of months I spent most of my life horizontal, being rotated from my side to back to other side like a barbecuing chook, viewing the world through the curved mirror. I could always tell when my occupational therapist was coming – she had a really funny laugh and very distinct walk. Things as simple as the way someone walked set them apart. It was a far cry from the vast open outback to the confines of a small mirror in a spinal unit in a big city.

My time in the spinal unit was like climbing a ladder. Each rung was another step towards getting home, and brought a huge sense of achievement. My first major step was getting out of traction – which meant getting the skull tongs out of the sides of my head.

If I had the same injury today, I'd be operated on and be up and about in a wheelchair within a week or two. Back in the 1980s, it took much longer. For eight long weeks I'd been living with the skull tongs and associated weights on my head. Every time they moved me it was painful – and the regular turning in bed was the most painful of all. Eating and any other motion also hurt as the wounds where the tongs were attached to my skull remained tender and sore, unable to heal because of the constant movement. I couldn't wait to get the skull tongs removed. I'd been looking forward to it for days. It didn't take staff long to free the tongs and, thankfully, it hardly hurt at all. It was a great relief.

But I'd jumped out of the pot into the fire. The traction was replaced by a SOMI brace. SOMI is an abbreviation for sterno-occipital-mandibular immobiliser, sterno meaning upper and midchest, occipital for base of skull, mandibular for chin and jaw and immobiliser meaning giving support and preventing movement of body parts. It was a frame that provided a rigid support for my spine and head, supported by padding strapped around my chest. It had three arms, one supporting my chin and the others supporting the back of my head.

How my chin itched! If I hadn't shaved for even a couple of days, it was excruciating. All I wanted to do was scratch. The only time the SOMI brace's chin piece was removed was to let me shave first thing in the morning before I got out of bed. What a relief, as temporary as it was. I still couldn't move my head and I had to wear the new brace all the time, even when I slept. Sometimes I thought I'd rather have stayed in traction. The only bonus was knowing it was a step in the right direction and I could finally get up, although that posed a whole new challenge.

I'd been lying on my back so long that I couldn't sit up without becoming so dizzy I passed out. The blood in my body had been pooling to the lowest point due to gravity for the past eight weeks and consequently I'd lost the muscle and blood vessel tone that normally pumps it back up when you stand. While that tone would return over time, when I first started getting up there would be a sudden rush of blood and my head would start spinning. It was an awful feeling, knowing I was fainting. I'd pass out and the staff would tip me back and gradually I'd come round. Then I'd try again. They'd lift the bed again, and I'd fight the dizziness. Eventually, I could sit up in bed without passing out. It was another tiny step up the ladder.

Once I could sit up it was fantastic. Finally, I could see the faces of the people I'd grown to know in the oval mirror over my bed, the staff who had helped me get to that point and the other patients I'd met. Seeing the world from an upright position, I discovered my horizontal perception of people was totally at odds with reality. The spinal unit, my room – everything was incongruous. I'd heard people telling me about the acute ward, wards two, three and four and the gym and occupational therapy room. I'd painted in my mind what I thought they looked like, but they were totally different when I got up.

I had the room sizes right in my mind, but nothing was where I thought it was. Each ward had four beds, two against opposite walls. A doorway entered from the spinal unit hallway, and straight ahead the outside wall contained a glass sliding door which opened onto a balcony. People talked about the nurses' station – and I'd imagined where it was. But it was nowhere near where I'd thought. So in a sense, I entered a whole new world.

And I was incredibly weak. I'd push myself around in my chair for five minutes and I'd be stuffed. Being paralysed from the chest down, just holding myself up in the wheelchair was exhausting. I couldn't believe how much strength it took to sit up in the chair, even with a strap around my chest and a chair with high sides.

But I was determined to climb that ladder as fast as I possibly could. Next I had to get into a sitting position by myself. First I learnt different ways to sit up, rolling over to each side while lying on a gym mat on the floor. Gradually, with practice and weight training to build up the strength in my arms, I learnt to sit up in bed by myself. It took me a whole week. Whenever I was thinking of giving up, I'd look across at Gary in the bed beside me, waiting for someone to help him. I would see him watching me. I'd try again.

Next I had to be able to get myself dressed. Before I started to get up, I'd been naked with only my teds and a sheet for modesty. There was probably a period of three weeks when I had lots of help to get dressed, in a simple tracksuit and sloppy joe, but then they threw me into the deep end. I can't even start to tell you how difficult it was to pull pants onto legs that I couldn't feel and that refused to co-operate, or to pull on a top when I had only two arms to balance a torso that couldn't hold itself up. I was like a table with three wobbly legs swaying in the wind. Crashes were par for the course.

Then I learnt to transfer from my bed to my wheelchair and back, and from my bed to my bathchair and back. To begin with, I lost my balance all the time, but in the spinal unit there was always someone there to grab me and stop me falling.

Combing my hair was a nightmare. I didn't actually have enough strength in my hand to hold the comb, so staff made a mould to fit into my hand and attach to the comb. It was such a tiny, insignificant everyday task, yet such a huge mountain to climb.

Even something as simple as brushing my teeth was suddenly a marathon in determination, requiring considerable ingenuity. I had trouble squeezing the toothpaste out of the tube and I certainly couldn't hold the toothpaste in one hand and the toothbrush in the other. I would put the tube on the side of the bench and push down with my good right hand until a little bit of toothpaste hung suspended from the tube. The idea was to then pick up the toothbrush and wipe the suspended toothpaste from the end of the tube before it dripped onto the floor. If it did, I'd have to start again. If the paste dropped onto the bench, I'd scrape it up from there with my toothbrush. I wasn't using my left hand at all, doing it all with my weak, inflexible right hand. On a bad day I'd drop my toothbrush. I'd never picked up anything off the ground so I had to find someone to pick it up for me. Then I'd start all over again. It could take half an hour to clean my teeth. Much later, after going home, I taught myself to use that left hand but in the days in the spinal unit I didn't have the skill.

Getting myself around in my wheelchair required a feat of athletic proportions, balancing my unstable torso while I pushed, and the first time I reached out to shake someone's hand I almost fell flat on my face. Little things like that had become a whole different ball game. My brain still tried to do things the old way, but it didn't work any more. My computer program was well and truly out of date.

At first I was totally disorganised and I'd leave half my clothes where I couldn't reach them in the morning. I'd sit up in bed, prepare to dress myself and my tracksuit pants would be over on the shelf out of reach. So I soon learnt to get everything ready for morning the night before. Often, just when I thought I was starting to get on top of things, something would go wrong. While I was putting on my shoes, I'd drop one off the side of the bed and have to call out for someone to pick it up. I'd try again. It was enormously frustrating.

The final rung on the spinal unit ladder was learning to negotiate the outside world. It was part of my rehabilitation process virtually from the time I could sit up in a wheelchair, but was the most difficult task to master. It was a big shock, taking my wheelchair outside for the very first time. Until then, I had no idea of the challenges involved. The unit was plain sailing. It was all set up with even, smooth floors, low-rising ramps, large open spaces and wide doorways. It had no stairs or lips or twigs or stones to trip you up. Nothing prepared me for all this. When I headed outside, I found myself in my own personal horror obstacle course. It was terrifying.

On my first outdoor session, all I did was go across the street to the café, chemist and shops. It was the little things that threw me. When I went to push the pedestrian button at the traffic lights, I nearly fell out of my chair. There was a ledge onto the roadway, a tiny drop of merely four or five centimetres. It may as well have been Niagra Falls. 'How do I get down there?' I wondered.

There was really no choice. I either let things like that stop me or I threw caution to the wind and had a go. So I pushed like hell and hoped it would be all right. I made it across the road without plastering my forehead in asphalt. What a sense of relief. That first time was terribly scary but it became easier after that.

I wheeled down the footpath and hit a small stick. It was tiny, just a twig, but my wheelchair lurched and I nearly went flying. I clung to my chair for dear life.

I was thinking, 'This is a nightmare.'

Everywhere I looked there was something in the way, something that could send me sprawling. My brain thought, 'Go down the street, go to the café and chemist ... piece of cake.' My brain didn't consider accessibility and shelf heights and sticks and stones.

One day they gave me a series of chores. I had to go to the bank and collect a deposit slip, go to the café and order a pie, and finally, go the newsagency and buy a magazine. I left the safe confines of the hospital feeling petrified.

Gingerly, I wheeled down the footpath, watching for branches or twigs on the cement. I braced myself with my right arm, as I reached for the pedestrian button. No way was I making that mistake again! I managed to get across the street and wheeled up to the bank. Thank goodness there was a ramp. I pushed my chair to the base, but it was too steep. I couldn't possibly push myself up. The café and newsagency were the same, they all had ledges or obstacles of some sort.

I asked someone to give me a push up into the newsagency and then I spent the whole time worried about how I was going

56

to get out. Like a cat that had climbed a tree but then couldn't get back down again. Where was the rescue team?

I bought a magazine and headed for the ledge at the doorway. I pushed, trying to balance as the wheels left the floor. I fell. The one good thing about falling out of a wheelchair is the fact that it's usually pretty graceful. Slow motion. I just plopped out. I didn't hit the ground like a ton of bricks. As I fell forward I broke the fall with my arms and hands. So much for trying to be independent. A couple of people raced to help me. They dusted me off and helped me back into my chair. I was so embarrassed.

Dejected, I went back to the unit. Mission impossible. I hadn't completed any of the tasks without mishap. But one thing saved me from total dejection that day. I knew that everyone else in the unit had similar stories to tell. We were all in this together and fighting the same battles. We turned our mishaps into funny stories and we shared the road to recovery and independence.

As time went on, I still thought occasionally I was back in the Territory, but not so often and gradually even my dreams and waking moments were firmly cemented in the hospital walls. I was starting to settle into the pattern of my new life.

Each morning between 7.30 and 8am a nurse would walk into the ward and turn on the light. 'Wakey, wakey,' she called and my day would begin.

One or two nurses were assigned to each ward for every shift. The first thing my nurse would do was drain my overnight catheter bag. She'd give me a glass of water and have a chat before the lady with the pill trolley came around with my medicine. I was taking three different types of tablet, one to thin my blood, another to control muscle spasm and another to keep my bladder clean.

Another nurse pushing a trolley would collect a blood sample from the artery on the soft inside of my elbow. The daily testing was essential to make sure my blood wasn't clotting but all the needles became very painful. After a couple of months in the unit, I felt like a well-used pincushion. One morning when the nurse came in to collect my blood I couldn't bear it any longer. 'Please take the blood from somewhere else today,' I pleaded. 'Can you take it from somewhere I can't feel?' For two days she tried her best to take a sample from my feet, but then she couldn't pick up a blood vessel and had to go back to my arms.

After the blood tests, breakfast arrived. Generally, it was cereal and a bit of fruit. Often by then someone in the ward – which had four beds – had turned on their radio or stereo. It was the late 1980s, and these days, whenever I hear music from bands like Crowded House or Dire Straits it takes me back to that time in my life.

Then the process of getting up began. I usually had a shower at night, so after breakfast was cleared away, it was time to get up. My nurse helped me dress and get into my chair, until later on when I had mastered the skills myself. Even then, someone was always nearby in case of the inevitable crashes. There was always somebody around to help pick you up. In the early days, getting dressed seemed to take forever. In fact, I began to wonder if the rest of my entire life was going to consist of dressing and toileting.

The physio or OT often came to get me by mid-morning and my training continued. Physiotherapy involved sessions in the gym or pool, developing my strength and agility, wheelchair skills and techniques for sitting up and rolling over. Occasionally it included a trip down Ipswich Road. Occupational therapy normally took place in a room with a kitchen and other household items. I learnt to cook, use a computer and a knife and fork again. I worked on developing my hand strength and flexibility. It was all aimed at making me as independent as possible when I returned home.

Every Monday morning my doctor visited. With my physio-therapist, OT and a senior nurse, they huddled around my bed discussing my progress.

At lunchtime, when I was up in my chair, I'd have my meal in the dining room. In the afternoon there'd be a couple more sessions with the physio or OT, or sometimes there might be a talk to the whole unit about driving, or managing bladder and bowel. Mum and Dad often came to those talks, after which we would discuss modifications at home and the equipment I was going to need.

Each day was slightly different, and there was never a dull moment. Obviously it was that way to stop me sitting, looking into space, dwelling on my situation too much. After dinner in the dining room, I'd watch television or catch up with friends or family. By 8pm I'd climb back into bed, undress, get into a shower chair, have a shower, clean my teeth and be back in bed an hour-and-a-half later. To think I used to be able to do all that in less than fifteen minutes.

In the earlier weeks and months I remember being exhausted by the end of the day. Almost before my head hit the pillow I'd be asleep. It didn't stop the dreams, but as time passed there were fewer and fewer.

The pattern of the days was also broken by the occasional social outing or driving lesson. I'd go to the pub for lunch, or to the movies – either with the hospital staff and other patients, or friends and family. Kim McConville, Richard Browning and a few other mates were with me on one of my first trips out of the hospital. We went to the Red Brick Hotel not far from the PA, and down the road from Boggo Road gaol, which was still open at the time.

It was a pretty dodgy pub. It was all very loud and full of laughter. We drank, not excessively, and then suddenly I realised my catheter bag was full. Everyone had had enough beers to turn the whole thing into a joke. Someone yelled, 'Take cover, it's going to blow.' They dropped, pushing chairs over to protect themselves from the shrapnel of the pretend blast, almost wetting themselves from laughing so hard. We all were.

Finally, after everyone had recovered, Richard and Scott wheeled me into the men's toilets. I was trying to tell them what to do, fighting to stay upright in my wheelchair at the same time. It was still early days, and I was still wearing a torso belt.

Things unravelled from there. Richard picks up the story: 'We had a totally distended bladder bag, a wobbling jack-in-a-box sitting on immovable hips in a chair that kept rolling around with a voice that just kept getting louder and more confident with "the answer" just as the solution slipped out of our fingers. Scott and I each took turns at rolling around on the toilet floor holding our sides as a staff member entered to check what all the fuss was about – of course making it just all the funnier. Finally we got a plan: push Sam as close as we could to the aluminum water wall, unplug the bottom end of his catheter bag and send it down the wall. Well, that was what we'd hoped.

'Handling a bomb that seemed set to burst at any moment made the task extremely difficult to handle. That and the eerie warmth of the thing made it all creepy and funny at the same time. Cracking the lid was tough and with such pressure the yellow river shot out like a fire hydrant spurting all over the place, soaking my hands and feet. It was a desperate state of hilarity where one paralytic man in a chair was accompanied by two others paralytic with laughter and struggling to stay on their feet whilst trapped by a floor that was too sodden now to roll around on and recover. You, Sam, were very much to blame and seemed to be the one laughing loudest.

'When we finally returned to the spinal unit, we were all like chastened choir boys who had been muted by a collective shame. We couldn't tell anyone at first because, well, we felt stupid that we hadn't really considered the consequences.'

It didn't worry me. Times like these helped lift my spirits and are fond memories I still have today.

Richard Browning said something interesting one day. He said, 'I remember playing first fifteen rugby in 1985. I had had troubles with my shoulder dislocating and had just returned to play. I was set up by someone inside, who made me look good by going over in the corner. But I got an extremely heavy tackle and you, Sam, picked me up and said something like: "Woo hoo, your shoulder must be all good now after that." I nodded and ran back with you and others to set up for the next play, all the while my shoulder was killing me and my ribs were screaming.

'I wonder how much screaming went on, on the inside for you, Sam. We had such fun together, but the quietness, the other side of our leaving was something you had to live with all by yourself. Whether we were family, friend, relative, we all walked out sometime or other, leaving you alone. I wonder how much screaming went on in the inside.'

It's true. Everyone else did get to walk out of the hospital door at the end of each day and go home. We'd had our fun and laughter, but in the end it did come down to just me. In the end, I had to find the strength to go on deep within myself. Nobody else could do it for me.

Until I faced quadriplegia, I never knew if I had that strength. Thankfully, I dug down deep and found I could cope. When I was alone, I didn't dwell on my situation. To be perfectly honest, most of the time I was too tired. And I always knew that tomorrow, there'd be more visitors. Kim or Richard or Mum and Dad, or other friends and family would walk through the door again. Next time Richard came he'd bring another carload of raucous mates to brighten my day. Who would have thought, that day I picked him up on the rugby field and gave him support way back in 1985, that one day he'd be doing the same for me. Life has a funny way of turning out.

For many years Mum kept to herself one incident that happened in those early weeks. Neither Kate, Bill nor I were aware of it but at about this time Mum discovered a lump in her breast. Her first reaction was to do nothing. 'God, we've got enough on our plate,' she said. But Lee, her ever-supportive sister-in-law, would have none of it. She made an appointment for Mum with her GP in St Lucia, a nearby suburb. As they sat in the waiting room, Mum's armour plating finally started to crack.

'And what's your problem?' asked the doctor.

Tears welled. 'I think I've got a lump in my breast,' she managed to blurt out before the floodgates opened.

He found her a box of tissues and she grabbed a handful. 'I'm sorry about this,' she said.

'Don't worry. Are you in Brisbane for this reason?'

'No. My son's had an accident.'

'Oh dear. I hope it's nothing serious.'

'He's a quadriplegic.' Once more she dissolved into floods of tears.

'Have you cried about it before?'

'No.'

'Well, then – it's about time you did,' he told her. 'Go for your life.'

Fortunately the lump was benign.

FIVE

MY DREAM COMES TRUE

As far back as I can remember all I've ever wanted was to be a farmer – just like my dad. I used to come home from primary school and throw my school bag onto the verandah. I'd down a glass of Milo with a Scotch Finger biscuit, then put on my work clothes and my plaited belt, with its pocket knife and various other things attached. I'd grab my hat, whistle my dog and I'd be off to see what Dad was doing. And that's how my childhood was. Virtually from the time I could walk I went everywhere with him, in my riding boots and floppy hat. I even stood the way he did – hands on hips with the fingers turned under. If he took his shirt off, so did I.

He drove an old white Holden Belmont ute around our 1460-hectare farm near Croppa Creek. The first time I drove Dad's old ute I was six or seven. He'd pulled up to open a gate and I thought, 'Here's my chance.' I slid across the old vinyl bench seat, positioning myself behind the steering wheel and perched on the edge of the seat, stretching my toes as far as possible to

64

push in the clutch. My head was level with the gearstick on the steering column. I pulled it into first. I then had to work myself upright as much as possible to see over the dashboard.

But my foot slipped off the clutch. The car lurched forward like a dog lunging at the end of its leash. Not only did I nearly take out the gatepost, Dad just about went under as well. After that I practised my driving skills on the airstrip, a flat, slashed area in front of the house.

One day Mum, Dad, my mum's aunt Molly and Dick Hodgkinson – a leading Sydney orthopaedic surgeon who loved nothing more than getting his hands dirty in the bush – were sitting on the front verandah. As they sat relaxing and chatting, the utility went past on the airstrip.

Dick exclaimed, 'There's nobody in that ute!'

'Yes, there is,' said Mum. 'It's Sam.' Sure enough, a few seconds later my head appeared above the dashboard like a jack-in-the-box as I stretched myself up to see where I was going. Then I disappeared again to concentrate on the accelerator and control the steering wheel.

On another occasion Dick watched as my younger brother Bill and I drove our bikes Evel Knievel-style up and down the banks of the house dam. Dick, whose business it was to repair shattered bones, shook his head in disbelief. 'You know, they'll be terrific kids,' he said, adding dryly, 'if they survive!'

I was that kind of kid. Into everything. I suppose I was an adventurer and nothing seemed impossible. Perhaps I was a little reckless too. Bill reckons as a child I led him astray, getting up to no good around the farm. He was probably right. I wasn't afraid of very much.

Now I look back and think what a fantastic childhood I had. There was such freedom, hundreds of hectares to explore. I loved being outside in the open air, the horizon miles away in the distance. There was sunshine and fresh air and the wind in my face. I wasn't a reader or television watcher. I liked to feel dirt on my hands. I liked building things. I loved the animals, the machinery, the crops, the bush and the creek. They were some of the things I treasured about growing up on our farm. I loved the tilling of the soil, the growing of the crop, the fascination of how everything worked. That was the love affair – the fact you could plant a seed and it would grow into a plant and produce grain. It was the nurturing of it, spraying it and finally harvesting it.

I spent hours riding on the mudguard of the tractor while Dad was driving, waiting for those precious occasions when he would say, 'Would you like to have a steer?' That's all it took – a few moments – to keep me waiting like a worm on a hook.

Rainy days were bliss. I'd go down to the dam and watch the torrent of water flowing in. I'd build little gullies, like the banks in the cultivation paddocks, and watch the water changing direction. I'd build elaborate rafts and float them on the dam.

I can still picture my first billycart. Dad helped me make it. We took the wheels and axles off an old pram and welded on a couple of attachments for two slabs of wood. We then knotted a length of rope onto each end of the front axle and I was in heaven. It went like the clappers, especially when we towed it behind the motorbike.

With a forked stick and a couple of rubber bands, I built a slingshot. With practice I could hit a moving target a few metres away. The main victim was of course Bill, who wasn't impressed until he built one too.

I loved the wildlife, the kangaroos, the emus, the birds, even the snakes. My best mate, Jamie Donaldson, lived next door. We used to meet down on the banks of Croppa Creek and go fishing, catching craybobs, exploring and rabbit trapping. We'd spend hours together and return to our respective homes covered in mud and grime.

I remember the first rifle I shot. I often kept Dad company when he went shooting and one day we were walking through the scrub when we came to a dam. A stick was poking up from the water and Dad said, 'See if you can hit that.' I lined up the sights on the .22 rifle, resting the butt against my shoulder. I pulled the trigger, bracing against the kick-back, missing by a mile. I didn't care. I still felt a sense of satisfaction and felt so grown-up. I was seven.

When I was a bit older, I often went shooting with Jamie. Feral pigs were our main target and the day we got our first big boar we had our photos taken with one foot firmly planted on his lifeless body like the big game hunters we were.

Another memory is the first time I used a chainsaw, cutting up a bit of firewood with Dad. I'd watched my father do it a hundred times. It was so exciting finally doing it myself. I tugged the starter cord and the engine throbbed instantly. I could feel the power of the engine vibrating through my hands as the teeth of the chain bit into the wood, and the smell of the sawdust floating in the air.

A favourite pastime was finding out how things worked and why they worked. It's hardly surprising that I was good at pulling things apart. I wasn't so successful at putting them back together but thankfully I got better at that over time.

As I grew older, the things that attracted me to farming changed. By the time I was in my teens I was drawn to the country way of life, being my own boss and being in charge of my own destiny. I wanted to work with nature and produce something that people needed.

I also enjoyed the physical work and the knowledge that I was making a difference. I took pleasure in something as menial as picking up rocks. In my mind, I wasn't picking up rocks, I was cleaning up the paddock and improving the land so I could plant a crop. I got great satisfaction out of things like that. They gave me a sense of achievement, the feeling that I'd left my mark on the landscape.

After primary at Croppa Creek Public School – where there were two teachers and about thirty kids from Kindergarten to Grade 6 – I went away to board at The Armidale School, about three hours' drive southeast of home.

In the first year or two I was a bit homesick but I toughed it out and never cried. I was always pretty stoic; that was how I handled the things that happened later in my life.

Mum used to say, 'Sam would never let you see him cry but Bill and Kate preferred to let you know when they were miserable.' As a child, Bill would cry at the drop of a hat and when Kate went to boarding school she bombarded Mum and Dad with tearful phone calls and distraught letters for most of her first term.

By the time I got to the last two or three years, school was phenomenal. Dad often said, 'Sam's going back to the country club.' He was pretty right. I had a terrific mob of mates and we shared a dislike of all things academic and a passion for sport, fun and adventure. We thought lessons were just a drag.

I lived in Tyrell House, one of four boarding houses at TAS. My house master Jim Graham, known as Jungle, was pretty quick to sum up the inner workings of most boys and there wasn't much we could put over him. Obviously we tested him to the limit but I owe him a lot and he remains one of my closest friends.

It was Jungle who convinced me that there was more to life than rugby and who eventually coaxed me onto the stage in a couple of his end-of-year productions. I played The Tramp in *Salad Days* and later Private Willis in Gilbert and Sullivan's *Iolanthe*, when I marched about the stage in the scarlet jacket and bearskin of the Grenadier Guards and, much to the amusement of my rugby mates, I sang a solo. Later it was Jungle who gave me another role at school. He appointed me house captain, which I loved although it was a delicate balancing act. On the one hand I had to wear the responsibility tag and on the other I enjoyed being one of the boys.

We got up to a fair few things that our parents and probably a lot of other people didn't know about. A couple of mates and I – we called ourselves the Three Musketeers – would sneak off at night after rollcall. With the whole night ahead of us, we had many adventures. The drive-in theatre was just up the road east of the school and we worked out that late at night they showed some pretty interesting stuff. We found an old hayshed on the other side of the road from the screen and we used to cycle out there, sit up on top of the haystack, sipping cheap flagon port and smoking Winfields, watching the movies. At that age, it was a great night's entertainment. Meanwhile the staff thought we were tucked in bed. At least that's what we believed at the time. Jungle told me years later he suspected there were things going on.

He also said he had given me the house captain's job with some reservations. 'As far as school and normal regulations went, Sam was a breaker of rules and laws, but on the surface, he was a conformist. He was smart enough to keep his nose clean and not get caught.

'But even though he wasn't caught, I'd have to be pretty dumb not to know he was up to all sorts of things. The fact he was so popular and readily accepted as a leader amongst boys meant there was also the streak of the daredevil there, because they liked the larrikin. I wanted to encourage the larrikinism, which was a wonderful trait, but on the other hand, I had to come down on rule breakers and not let them run riot.'

We found a cherry farm not far out of town and went on nocturnal expeditions out there to sample the cherries. No doubt they tasted even nicer because they were stolen. The owner never caught us, but one of the funniest things was that one of the Musketeers was going out with his daughter.

It was all pretty harmless fun. I remember we found a manhole in the floor of our prep room and discovered we could get down there and go under all the school. We used to call it going underground. We acquired pairs of overalls to wear over our school clothes to keep them clean and when we were supposed to be doing prep, the three of us would be exploring the murky underground of the school buildings, among the spider webs and dirt and dust. It was lots of fun.

I was part of a TAS rugby team that toured the British Isles in 1984. It was an amazing trip. Imagine thirty school kids, ranging from sixteen to eighteen years of age, let off the chain and gallivanting around the world together. The fun and experiences we had on that trip and the bond we established will be with us for the rest of our lives. The driving force behind the trip was our rugby coach, Ken McConville, and one of our teachers, John Hipwell, was tour manager. He'd played for the Wallabies and had been on several overseas tours with them, so knew all the shortcuts. He said our tour had many similarities, in the sightseeing we did and where we played.

The following year we were the most successful rugby team that had ever represented TAS. We were undefeated and I think it was because of the experience we gained on that tour. We were also spurred along by the tragic death of Ken McConville, in an abseiling accident three months prior to our first game. We even beat Sydney's St Joseph's College, and they weren't used to losing. In fact, a well-known Armidale businessman had promised he would shout the whole school ice-cream and fruit salad if ever TAS beat Joeys. He was true to his word, and the following day all the boys sat in the school dining room and polished off their special treat.

My other major interest during my later years at school was girls. I knew my way over to the girls' boarding schools, NEGS and PLC, blindfolded. From Year 10 onwards, I was often seeing someone. In Year 12 I had a girlfriend on one side of town and a classmate, Jock Hudson, had one on the other. Once we had our driver's licences, Jungle lent us his car to visit our girlfriends. Even better, whenever we got into the car it was full of fuel. The car spent so much time going to and fro between our dates that Jungle nearly had to book to use it.

Meanwhile, there wasn't much studying going on. I wasn't interested in academic subjects and there were too many other more exciting things to do than spend time with my nose stuck in a book. One of my mates suggested a quick way to learn our English novels was to read the back cover, the first chapter and the first two paragraphs of every other chapter. It sounded like a good idea at the time but it didn't work and I failed English, along with most of my other subjects. My Higher School Certificate mark ruled me out of doing medicine or vet science. In fact, it ruled me out of most things. But while I didn't gain much academically from the classroom at TAS, they were some of the best years of my life and the values and friendships I gained will be with me forever.

If it had been left up to me, I would have left school early and come straight home to work on the family farm, but my parents insisted I go away and experience working and living somewhere else. Get out and see the world.

A cousin, Richard Smith, owned a property near Stonehenge, about 150 kilometres southwest of Longreach in central Queensland. He ran a cattle enterprise with his wife Sue, better known as Wapp, and also had a contract fencing business. I'd never met him but his story captivated me. What he'd done sounded adventurous and exciting so we got the map out and had a look at where Stonehenge was. It was miles from anywhere. My interest was well and truly aroused.

Mum gave him a phone call. I remember hearing her say, 'He's pretty green and loves a party ...' But I landed a job.

Dad obviously realised I was going to need some wheels of some sort, so he offered me his ute that had been a paddock basher for some years. Probably giving a fair bit of consideration to my HSC mark he wasn't going to splash out, so he gave this old thing a wash, took it into town and got it registered and presented it to me. I thought he'd given it to me, but he whispered in my ear just before I left that he'd like $1100 for it when I made my small fortune. Mind you, he must have known something I didn't because the bloody thing blew up not long after I got up there.

At any rate I had my wheels. I put in a tape deck and radio and added some big shiny spotlights on the front. The ute had a little sissy bullbar which I was pretty ashamed of but I didn't have the money to put a proper one on, so I had to be content with that. For a final touch, I drilled a couple of holes in the muffler to make it sound a bit beefier and I was ready to roll. It was a little battered and faded, but it was my pride and joy, my trademark. It was the car every country boy dreamt of.

At the end of January 1986 I packed all my meagre belongings into a suitcase – some work clothes, a couple of good shirts and better jeans, shaving cream, a razor, toothbrush, toothpaste and comb. That was about all I had, that and my swag, which I'd been given for Christmas – still all shiny and new. I put in a water bottle, a jerry can of fuel and an extra spare tyre. As daylight was seeping over the horizon, I climbed into my ute, a set of cassette tapes on the seat beside me.

I had a fair drive ahead of me and we worked out that if I left at four o'clock in the morning then I stood a fair chance of getting to Stonehenge before it got dark, allowing for a few stops along the way to get fuel and food. As I was about to drive out the gate Mum presented me with a map. I already had a road atlas and was baffled. What did I need another map for?

But her map showed the whole journey marked with a big black texta and she'd circled several major towns along the way. I thought, 'What's going on here?' She said, 'Ring me from these places please, Sam.'

'Oooh, Mum!' I protested.

'You don't have to talk to me, just find a phone box, pick up the phone and say Mitchell ... Augathella ... Blackall ... or whatever. Then at least if you don't arrive by tonight I'll have a rough idea of where to start looking.'

I'll never forget driving out the front gate that day. It was pretty daunting as the umbilical cord was finally being severed. I was moving a thousand kilometres away from home to live with people I'd never met. I felt scared but elated, fearful yet excited as I began the next chapter in my life. By the time I'd passed through the front gate my Jimmy Barnes tape was screaming and I was off.

It was a mammoth trip and the further north I went, the longer the distances stretched between towns. It was so different from what I'd grown up with – where you only drove a few kilometres to get to the next property and had a town or village every half hour. In southwest Queensland it's often an hour or more to the next town and there's little sign of life in between, just an occasional cattle grid and mailbox, sweltering in the heat and dust. As the sun climbed into the vast outback sky my vehicle felt like an oven, even with all the windows down to help circulate the hot air. No such thing as airconditioning in that old ute.

Finally I made it to Barcaldine and I thought, 'Only another hour to Longreach, I'm virtually there.' How wrong I was! When I turned off the highway to head southwest, the sign told me I still had 150 kilometres to go to Stonehenge. As I pushed on, I truly felt the remoteness stretching around me. Until then I'd been travelling along major highways and there had seemed to be some variation in the landscape, with patches of timber, occasional roadhouses and towns, and road trains passing by. I hadn't felt really alone until now.

The tar was replaced by a typical dirt road, and running through its centre was a huge crown, a mini mountain range caused by the constant use of trucks. Hoping my ute wouldn't lose its sump on the crown, I shuddered over the corrugates for more than two hours.

At last I arrived at Stonehenge in a cloud of bull dust as the sun sunk towards the west. Nothing like I'd imagined, it was a tiny village in the middle of nowhere. I could see immediately where it got its name because it was on top of a plateau. I drove down the main street – if you could call it that – with the odd house here and there, some abandoned and derelict.

I found the one and only pub and pulled up. I walked into the bar to find a gaggle of weathered stockmen drinking beer.

'G'day, how're you going?' I said to the barman.

'Yeh, good … can I get you something?'

'I was wondering if you could tell me where Richard Smith lives.'

'Richard Smith … who's Richard Smith?' he asked.

I explained he was a cousin of mine and he had a place around here somewhere.

He yelled out, 'Does anyone know a Richard Smith … do we have a Richard Smith around here somewhere?'

'Oh, Dick … yeah Dick … he lives about five miles up that way,' yelled one of the men at the bar, waving his arm to the north.

Wearily, I climbed back into the car and headed down the road as the sun was setting. My journey was almost over. I've never been so glad to see a signpost on a gateway. It read 'Depot Glen'. I drove in feeling like an old wornout stock saddle, covered in sweat and dust and feeling totally buggered.

I drove up to an old weatherboard house and pulled up. I saw a big, darkly tanned bloke, wearing work clothes, thongs and a big hat, heading in my direction. He was a tall, powerful-looking man and with some trepidation, I thought, 'I hope I've got the right place.'

Then out of the corner of my eye I spotted another figure coming towards me. As it got closer, I saw long hair and thought it must be Wapp. She was coming from the direction of some horses and what I assumed must have been stables. As she got closer and said gidday, I glanced down and saw that her feet were bare, even though she'd just walked across the paddock. And she'd obviously taken a shortcut through the chook yard, because all the evidence was oozing up between her toes. I'll never forget that as long as I live. In a way it was comforting. All the way up I'd been thinking I'd better be polite and not cough and burp and carry on like I did at home. But now, instantly, I knew I could be myself. An awkward barrier was immediately broken.

In fact, I grew to think the world of Dick and Wapp. He was salt of the earth, with a passion for the outback, a wonderful storyteller and hard worker. Wapp was also a toiler and heaps of fun.

My year at Depot Glen was fantastic, although it didn't get off to a very good start. I was as green as buggery and it showed the very first morning. Dick told me we were going out fencing on the northern end of the 12,500 hectare property. That wasn't just down the road – it took more than half an hour to get there.

He asked me to get all the fencing equipment, the wire strainers, the crowbar, the shovel and then go to the woodheap and throw a couple of old strainer posts onto the back of the ute as well. One of the posts was lodged in between a couple of rails, so I got the crowbar out of the back and used it to pry it loose. I loaded the posts, picked up Dick and we headed out to the boundary fence. After a bit of preparation, Dick asked me to get the crowbar and shovel to dig a hole for the strainer posts. I walked over to the ute and suddenly I froze – no crowbar. I could clearly visualise the dark steel bar lying beside the woodheap. I'd forgotten to load it back into the ute.

So I had to go back, with my tail between my legs and tell Dick, 'You're not going to believe this, I've left the crowbar back at the house.'

Without the corner post, we had nothing to attach the fence to. We couldn't do a thing. We'd brought our lunch, ready for a full day's work, but we didn't need it. We drove all the way home with me sitting there thinking, 'You dickhead, you absolute dickhead!' Thankfully, I got better.

The year I was working on Depot Glen we built hundreds of kilometres of fencing. At the time the Australian government was trying to eradicate tuberculosis in the country's cattle herd and many of the big outback stations were putting up boundary fences for the first time so they could muster and destroy any cattle carrying the disease.

We did a lot of fencing on a property called 'Connemara', where an internal fence alone stretched 30 or 40 kilometres, and that was just one of the small paddocks. First a dozer would clear a track, the width of a tennis court. These tracks cut a swathe through bushland in a straight line as far as the eye could see. Workmen would light a rubber tyre in the distance, and the dozer would head straight for the smoke, and then they'd do another one and another. That was the crude but effective way of surveying the line. I remember coming to a rise, or jump up, as they were known in the outback, and seeing this cleared line stretching for kilometres in front of me. It seemed to go forever and it was incredibly daunting knowing we had to put a fence up along that entire distance. For a moment I understood how the pioneers must have felt as they settled the vast outback.

First we cut all our strainer posts and stays from the local gidgee and mulga trees, much as the early white settlers would have done. We'd spend a day just cutting posts, only we used a chainsaw when they would have used an axe and handsaw. We loaded them onto a bogey trailer capable of carrying hundreds of steel posts and a number of wooden strainers as well. Then we'd lay the posts along the line. We had a bit of wire trailing on the ground behind the trailer, with a weight on the end. When it passed the previous post I'd throw out another one while Dick kept driving. After ten steel posts we'd stop and Dick would help me unload a wooden post. We'd set off again.

Then we'd go back along the line putting in the posts. We used a posthole digger for the wooden strainers, but the steel posts were put in by hand using a dolly — a round cylinder that went over the top of the posts with handles on either side. You'd grip the handles and dong the iron posts into the ground. That could sometimes be a real challenge. There was a lot of what they call top rock in that country. The first few hits on the steel post would drive it in easily but then you'd hit rock and the dolly would just bounce. It was heartbreaking. It didn't matter how hard you rammed down the dolly, the steel post didn't budge. Thankfully Dick had a big rock drill powered by a two-stroke motor, similar to the one used on roadworks. It had a drill bit on the end, almost a metre in length, which cut through the rock. It was still painstakingly slow but you knew once the posts were in, they would never move. We built a suspension fence, with three barbed wires strung twenty-five metres between each steel post. Each span was then supported by two steel droppers – which thankfully didn't have to go into the ground. We averaged about three kilometres a day and would live on the fenceline for a week or so.

I loved living in the bush with Dick. Our camp included an old caravan that served as the kitchen and stored our belongings and food. We had a big gas fridge for the beer, a smaller one for our perishable food – and fresh meat was delivered regularly by the station manager. We cooked on a campfire, using a charred, well-seasoned camp oven and barbecue. At night we'd sit around the campfire and I'd listen to Dick's stories about living and working in the Northern Territory, Kimberleys and Gulf Country, where sometimes he was the only white man on the station. He kept me entertained for hours. Not that we'd stay up late. Most nights we'd shower under a canvas bag shower hung up in a tree, have something to eat and fall into our swags exhausted.

We worked hard and long hours. Often our campsite would be as far as ten kilometres from our fence, so we'd be up well before daylight to have breakfast and be ready to start at first light. Some days we'd work until we could no longer see the posts and wire in the growing darkness. In summer the days were even longer and we sweated like pigs in the heat as temperatures rose to 40 degrees Celsius and more. I very quickly learnt not to leave my dolly lying in the sun after I almost burnt myself picking it up a couple of times. I was also forever losing my pliers and a couple of other things. Dick must have had a few chuckles to himself in those early days.

After we'd been working on Connemara's internal fences for a few months, Dick tendered to do the whole boundary. It stretched something like 200 kilometres and took us a whole day to drive its entire length. I felt sick at the thought of having to build a fence that long. The fencing materials arrived on a road train groaning under the weight of many palettes of barbed wire and slings of steel posts. Each sling was made up of 400 posts. As we unloaded them, I thought to myself, 'You stupid bastard. You've got to put all these in the ground.'

We completed that job while I was there, with the help of a couple of extra people, including my childhood mate and neighbour Jamie Donaldson. I can tell you, I felt a terrific sense of achievement when it was completed. To be able to look back down those long cleared lines and know the fence down the centre was put there with the help of my own hands was a feat I'll never forget.

Two or three weeks after arriving at Stonehenge I had my first trip to Longreach. I needed to set up a bank account to deposit my wages into and to buy a few more work clothes. Mum and Dad had given me about $300 when I left home, to pay for fuel and food to get me to my new job and support myself until my first pay cheque. I had about $100 left. I thought I'd open a bank account, buy some work clothes, go to the pub for lunch, buy a magazine at the newsagency and head home. The day proceeded as planned. I opened the bank account and deposited about $40.

As I walked out of the bank I saw a menswear shop across the road. Perfect, I'd duck in there and buy some clothes. As soon as I walked in I spotted this great-looking girl at the counter and of course at that age I thought I was God's gift to the female race so I ruffled up my hair and undid the next button on my shirt and strolled in like King Tut. I picked out jeans, shorts and a handful of undies then swaggered over to the counter with my arms full.

'Gidday,' I said in the deepest voice possible. 'I'll take these, please.'

'Hello,' she said, smiling sweetly.

She was gorgeous. I watched her as she tallied up my bill, oblivious to the spiralling price as I planned my next move.

'That'll be ninety-three dollars, thanks,' she said.

I was stunned. I'm sure I turned green, which she probably didn't notice under my glowing tan. I stammered, I mumbled. I didn't know what to say. I had $60 in my wallet, if that. I hadn't thought to look at the price tags.

I can't remember now how I got out of it, but I limped dejectedly out of there with about four or five pairs of undies, a pair of shorts and my pride seriously dented. I had no money left for lunch or a magazine and I'd still be there if I hadn't happened to still have a full jerrycan of fuel in my ute, which was enough to get me back to Stonehenge.

I was learning the value of money the hard way. Welcome to the real world!

At the end of 1986, Dick and I chatted about what I planned to do the following year. He suggested working in the Northern Territory, where he'd spent many of his younger years. By then I'd fallen in love with the outback and jumped at the idea.

He was a friend of Geoff Wagstaff, the manager of Avon Downs at the time, and Dick contacted him to see if there was a job going. There was. I came home for Christmas and at the end of February 1987 I jumped back into the old ute and set sail to the Northern Territory for what I thought would be another fantastic adventure.

Again, I farewelled my family at Bardin and drove out over the front ramp with the music blaring. I wasn't quite so daunted by the journey this time but I had another map from my mother. Secretly, I was glad of that map and the phone calls because I was never quite sure if that old ute was going to get me there. I set off and crossed my fingers.

Four days later, after two unscheduled overnight stays as a result of rain-affected roads – it was still the wet season up north – I finally made it to the Northern Territory. As I drove steadily northwest, the landscape changed around me. The distances between the towns grew even longer and there was hardly any sign of life – just an occasional property entrance, sometimes displaying a name and the inevitable dusty mailbox. I rarely saw houses, sheds or other buildings. It was like driving into another land, even more remote than central Queensland.

As I drove, my sense of anticipation grew. There was a certain sense of homecoming, as I felt the isolation and vastness settling around me. I was so excited to be going back into the outback again – the distance stretching for lonely kilometre after kilometre.

It brought back memories of campfires and storytelling, and dingoes howling in the darkness as I lay in my swag at night. I recalled how occasionally the year before I'd find camel tracks going through the soft red sand. I'd leave behind my own footprint and wonder if any person – even an Aborigine – had ever walked on that piece of dirt before. I felt like an explorer walking through the last frontier and every day felt like an adventure. I was totally addicted.

Leaving behind Camooweal, the last town before Avon Downs, I drove across the Barkly Tablelands down a big, black line of a road that stretched to the horizon. The enormity of the landscape struck me. Everything seemed so big and even more remote than the country between Winton and Cloncurry.

Thirteen kilometres out of Camooweal I crossed the Northern Territory border. There was a big, imposing sign. It seemed to herald a new, thrilling chapter in my life. I could hardly contain my excitement. When I passed the Avon Downs airstrip, I knew my destination was getting close. I came to the entrance, the cattle grid and the signpost announcing 'Avon Downs' in big black letters.

Driving into the station, the layout was similar to most properties of that size in northern Australia. I drove down a couple of kilometres of dirt road leading to a cluster of buildings. A large main homestead, a few other outbuildings, cottages, the jackaroos' quarters and various other constructions formed a tiny township of their own.

I drove in and pulled up, easing my stiff body from the car. It was like stepping out onto a deserted movie set. But I could hear voices coming from a building and they led me to the kitchen and dining room, where everyone was eating their evening meal.

I introduced myself and two or three individuals came over immediately, shook my hand and introduced themselves. We settled into easy conversation about the weather, where we came from and things like that.

Again, the barriers instantly broke down. The station cook, Sunny, invited me to help myself to a meal and I joined them for dinner. There was an immediate bond. One of the other jackaroos led me to our quarters, a tidy, small fibro building with a tin roof. A set of steps led up into a hall with two rooms either side. Three were bedrooms and the fourth was a laundry and bathroom. Nearby another building had three bedrooms plus it had a lounge/TV room for the jackaroos.

It was simple, impersonal yet felt instantly like home. I threw my suitcase into one of the bedrooms where one of two single beds and a cupboard were to become my very own personal space. That was my home when we were at the station between stock camps.

About twenty-five people lived at Avon, including a team of jackaroos, station cook, head stockman and his wife, mechanic, a grader driver, windmill and bore expert and his family, and the manager, Geoff Wagstaff, his family and the governess, who taught his two children. Both the station cook and governess had their own separate quarters, the head stockman and bore mechanic and their families lived in separate houses, while the grader driver lived most of the time in a caravan out on the property where he was working. The station had a strong sense of family because the majority of us ate together most of the time. A horn would announce when meals were ready and everything was run with military precision.

Because we were seventy kilometres from the closest town there was also a station store, where we could buy bare essentials such as toothpaste and razors. It was run by each of the staff in turn, and when we bought something it was written up in a book and the cost taken out of our wages. My pay packet was next to nothing but I still managed to save some money because there was nowhere to spend it. When I was at the station, my wage also included a ration of beer, but the stock camp was dry.

When the station settled down to sleep at night, a peacefulness pervaded the landscape, marred by one constant noise only, the generator. Like a throbbing presence, it was always there in the background, providing power to the various buildings at Avon Downs. The only time we had total quiet was when it was turned off to be checked for oil or given a service and oil change. It took a bit of getting used to. For the first few nights I'd wake up in the darkness and think someone had forgotten to turn off the tractor.

Only one other noise ever marred the outback quietness and that was the occasional sound of traffic from the nearby Barkly Highway. At times, if the wind was in the right direction, we could hear the thunder of a road train – reminding us that we weren't completely alone, even out there in remote Northern Territory.

It was green and lush when I arrived at Avon towards the end of the wet season – a complete contrast to how it looked by the middle of winter, in the dry season when the landscape turned to virtual desert. For the first month we were confined to the station headquarters by the wet. We fenced, tidied up and painted the outbuildings until it was dry enough for the first stock camp to start.

We weren't idle. Most of us also had to master the art of horseriding. While I'd spent a little bit of time on a horse at the local bush pony club, I was far from a seasoned rider. And the thing about mustering on big stations like Avon Downs is you weren't just riding for half an hour. You were on these bloody horses all day. After the first day, I climbed off, bow-legged and crotchety as an old woman, with the inside of my calf muscles red raw where the hair and skin had rubbed against the saddle flaps all day. In the beginning, I could hardly walk after being on a horse but it got easier as time went along.

I was given a plant of four horses. The first plant included the oldest, quietest and, I discovered, most stubborn. Then I had to learn how to put shoes on their feet. I'd never shod a horse in my life before. It was so frustrating. One guy who had grown up in the Territory could run around and shoe a horse in less than an hour while I slaved away, taking hours for each individual shoe.

I wasn't alone either – there were five or six of us in the same predicament. The horses didn't help. They were wise, experienced animals who had trained a few other novices like me before and worked out a few tricks of their own. They'd lean all their weight on me, or pull their feet away or not stand still. It took me a whole bloody day to put shoes on one horse alone. My back was killing me and I had to shoe my whole team of four before the stock camp started! I thought I'd never get the hang of it but by the time I did the fourth one I'd figured out the basics – how to hold the leg, the right way to hammer the nails into the hoof and crimp them off properly.

But just when I thought I was making progress, I was given a fresh plant of far less experienced horses. The shoeing proved a whole new challenge all over again and I had to find a few different strategies for getting the job done. One horse I had hated having its back feet picked up, and it was pretty tough going, but I felt lucky compared with one of the other jackaroos. He had a horse that was so hard to shoe we had to throw it onto its side to put its hind shoes on. Eventually I could tap all four shoes on a horse in next to no time.

I'll never forget heading out to my first stock camp. I'd been looking forward to it for days. Avon Downs covered 393,900 hectares and there were several sets of cattle yards scattered across the station. Each yard serviced five or six paddocks. We'd camp at a set of cattle yards for eight to ten days while we mustered all the surrounding cattle for calf marking, weaning and TB testing. The entourage included the head stockman, eight jackaroos and the cook. We piled into and onto a Toyota trayback towing an old tin caravan and headed off followed by a motorbike and truck with dog trailer behind. The truck carried our thirty-six horses. In the sky overhead, a helicopter flew to meet us. It had been ordered a day or two earlier, flew into the station the day before the camp, came out to help us muster for a couple of days then left again. After driving for sometimes as long as an hour we would reach our destination, a set of cattle yards near a waterhole, a horse paddock and a strange steel frame standing lonely in the landscape. I climbed down from the back of the trayback and helped disconnect and set up the old caravan, which served as a bush kitchen, dining room and cook's quarters. One end had a stove and cooking area, the remainder was taken up with benches along the walls and a bench seat on the inside. An old electric refrigerator, powered by a generator, chugged away near the doorway keeping our food cool in the heat.

The low steel frame – a permanent fixture at each cattle yard on the station – consisted of six posts and an A-frame and covered about a quarter of the size of a tennis court. It revealed its purpose when we threw a tarpaulin over the frame and it became the roof on our makeshift jackaroos' quarters. It was pretty primitive with its dirt floor and open sides, but we had to keep it tidy. We slept in our swags on shearers' stretcher beds, four or five down each long side with enough space to walk down the centre. At night our clothes bags sat under our stretchers and each morning we rolled up our swags and placed them, with our bags, on top of the stretcher for the day. Our toileting was a basic affair. While the cook, Sandy, being the only female, got to use a shower at the back of the caravan, the rest of us washed in the turkey's nest, or a waterhole, or a trough.

Because we were basically on a flat plain, the turkey's nest was formed by building a circular wall above the ground level – a bit like a tank. The water came from a nearby bore, pumped by a windmill. The turkey's nest was fenced to keep out the stock and the water was gravity-fed to water troughs in surrounding paddocks. It was full of reeds, frogs, snakes and all sorts of things. We'd go for a swim every couple of days, clean up and then change our clothes.

The nights were cool in our open-sided sleeping quarters and I'd snuggle under the blankets and canvas cover of my swag, listening to the bellow of cattle locked in the yard overnight and croaks and rustles from the turkey's nest as I drifted off to asleep.

The stock camps were hard work. The days were long and exhausting. We'd often rise before daylight for breakfast. We'd muster the horses in the horse paddock with a motorbike, saddle

I was passionate about tilling the
earth, even at sixteen months.

My first day at Croppa Creek
Public School.

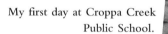

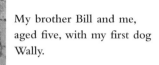

My brother Bill and me,
aged five, with my first dog
Wally.

All I ever wanted was to be a farmer just like my dad. I'm here with him and his business partner, Peter Jackes (right).

With Mum and Dad just before flying to the United Kingdom on my school rugby tour.

The 1985 TAS 1st XV undefeated rugby team (I'm front row, second from right).

Another never-ending fence line stretches into the distance. In 1986 Dick Smith and I fenced hundreds of kilometres of fence line on the property Connemara, in outback western Queensland.

Me (second from left) at the Tennant Creek Picnic Races in early 1987 with fellow jackaroo at Avon Downs, Steve Hagan (at my left).

Above: Celebrating my twentieth birthday in the spinal unit with chocolate cake served up by Kate while Dad looks on. I was still bedridden with skull tongs and looking at everyone in the curved mirror.

Right: Transferring into the Odyssey, my first big achievement.

Above: Taking out some frustration in the Honda Odyssey, my first form of mobility on the farm.

Left: Me with my ever-supportive parents, photographed on the front verandah of Bardin in 1991. (Photo: Mike Moores)

My great mate John Ryan helping me onto the tractor using my hoist.
(Photo: Mike Moores)

Me with my flying instructor Bruce McMullen after my first solo – with my
passenger, the bag of sand. (Courtesy *Warialda Standard*)

Doing a pre-flight check before takeoff in my Quicksilver MX2.
(Photo: Mike Lowe)

The ultralight was easy to get into – even for a quadriplegic.
(Photo: Mike Lowe)

up and load them onto a truck. We'd all climb in and drive for up to half an hour to the furthermost corner of the paddock and start mustering as the sun yawned slowly over the flat, vast horizon.

The sunrises were amazing. The dry, red plains – covered in scattered brown Mitchell grass – turned hot orange for a few glorious moments, and the sound of the helicopter chopped through the silence. Indelibly printed in my memory is the sight of stockmen riding through the dust behind the ever-growing mob of bellowing cattle as we pushed the cows and calves towards the yards.

Once they were mustered, the real work began as we marked calves, vaccinated everything, sorted older calves for weaning and collected blood samples from all the cows for TB testing. The camp was a hive of activity and there was often someone coming or going. Occasionally the head stockman would duck back to the station in the Toyota for something or the manager would drive out to check on how we were progressing.

Truckies in road trains arrived on cue to take away the weaners and a vet helped collect blood samples to be tested for TB. He returned a couple of days later with the results. Australia achieved Disease Free Status in December 1997 but a decade earlier any cattle found with TB were called reactors and had to be shot. Luckily, we didn't find many.

Most of the time we worked until dark but there were days when we got through our work earlier than expected, and that's when the real fun began. We'd run a few steers into the yards for our own personal rodeo. We entertained ourselves for hours by watching everyone get chucked off, yelling, clapping and laughing so hard we almost collapsed. We didn't have any hard hats or safety vests. Why we didn't get killed, I'll never know.

My four months at Avon Downs was a very special time of my life. I loved the way of life. It was like living in another land, experiencing a completely different culture. The people were down-to-earth, the landscape was vast and inviting – and I fell in love with them both. I made friendships that are still with me today.

While I don't think I would have spent the rest of my life there, at the time I was young, adventurous and energetic, and found it thrilling. By the middle of 1987 my life was going to plan. A couple of years of this, I thought, and then I'd go home to the family property and eventually take the reins from Dad. I'd get married, have kids, and the cycle would begin again.

That's how I envisaged my life would pan out. All I wanted to do was be on the land. There was no either/or, no second choice, that's all I wanted. That's how the picture looked from a very early age, and that's how it still looked by the middle of 1987. Six months later my dream came true. I arrived home, but not in my wildest dreams had I imagined I'd be confined to a wheelchair.

SIX

DARK DAYS

As long as I can remember, storms have rolled in from the west and drenched our family farm. In the sultry melting heat of a summer's day, dark clouds would build in the distance, stewing on top of each other higher and higher. The air grew heavy and moist. I could feel the excitement build as the storms grew closer. The wind eventually announced the splatter of rain. Trees danced wildly and the tin on the old sheds clapped at the sweet scents released from the earth. Then down came the soaking, drenching rain, so welcome. The weeks before my discharge from the spinal unit were a bit like a storm coming. Feelings of anticipation brewed on the horizon – getting closer and closer. I couldn't wait.

I'd already had my first taste of home at the end of November, and that had really whetted my appetite, even though it had been a bitter-sweet experience. It had been so good to be home in the country, in familiar surroundings, home with my family and to my mother's cooking. On the other hand, I had been intensely worried about getting pressure areas from sitting on my backside all the time. It's one of the things they taught me in the unit, to constantly relieve pressure on my rear end. We stopped on our way home three or four times, for me to lift up and take the weight off my bum. I was so paranoid that for the first part of the journey I sat on my wheelchair cushion on the front seat.

I was also worried because there seemed to be so much to remember, and it was the first time I had to do it all on my own without hospital staff to help. Like a kid studying my times tables, all the way home I went over and over in my mind what I had to remember, my routine … drugs … catheters. There had been a lot of fear and a lot of excitement.

The reason for my visit home was to attend a friend's twenty-first birthday party. It was to be the first time I saw many of my friends since we left school. I was really looking forward to it.

As Mum drove me and my girlfriend, Kim, to the party on a nearby property, all I could think about was catching up with my mates. But when I wheeled across the lawn, I was greeted with a deadly silence. No one seemed to know what to say or do. It was like time suddenly stood still as the reality of Sam in a wheelchair sunk in. It was obviously a hell of a shock to everyone. It was an even bigger shock for me. Suddenly I realised there was a lot more to being a quadriplegic than the physical disabilities.

Nobody had prepared me for this. There I was on the lawn, surrounded by the bar and seats and tables and everyone having a terrific time and suddenly it stopped, like a video on pause. There was some serious static happening here. All these good mates from school didn't know how to act, what to do. For me that moment stretched like the Grand Canyon but it was probably only a few seconds.

It took some older people to break the ice. They walked over and began chatting and gradually everyone started talking again. Slowly my mates found the courage to come and talk and discovered that I was still the same person inside my dramatically altered body. That night was a hell of a blow to me and I realised then that there would always be a wall between me and people who didn't know me, and even some who did. It is still the case today.

Did I enjoy the party? Yes and no. It was great to catch up with my school mates, including some of the schoolboy rugby team I'd toured the UK with in 1984, but it was also incredibly confronting and sobering to know that some people, even good mates, would struggle to come to terms with my injury and that for some our friendships would never be the same.

That first weekend I slept in the main house, not my old bedroom, which was in a separate building a few metres away. I had to be pulled up two steps into the house and the bed wasn't the right height, so we had to put a couple of house bricks under it to bring it up to wheelchair level. In those early days I was finding it difficult to turn over in bed at night so someone had to come and turn me over every couple of hours. The bathroom wasn't accessible but I coped for just two or three nights. It wasn't perfect – but it was good to be home.

Meanwhile, work had started on my new sleeping abode. My old bedroom and bathroom would have required too much modification to make it wheelchair-friendly so Mum and Dad decided to build something from scratch.

Mum, with her usual flair, gutted an old toolshed, meat house and laundry – which became my own personal verandah. Alongside this a cement slab was laid where my bedroom and bathroom would be built. Eventually they put in a walkway across to the house and a ramp up from the lawn. We called the pathway to the house 'Wombat Crossing' and I sat at the brink of each line of brickwork as it was being laid. It was wonderful when it was completed and I could finally come and go as I pleased between my bedroom and the main house. Don't get me wrong, Mum and Dad weren't trying to segregate me, they simply wanted to give me a bit of privacy, and I still used the house for everything apart from sleeping, showering and toileting.

By early December, there was still a long way to go to finish my new bedroom – a bit of a worry when I was coming home in a few weeks. But I wasn't thinking about that. All I could think about was getting back home so things could return to normal. At least that's what I thought.

The first trip home had been a success by spinal unit standards. I'd coped well and proved that I was almost ready to live independently of medical staff. It was then that they started talking to me about my future, what I might do with my life after I left hospital. Obviously, someone of my age still had their whole life ahead of them – and they felt that with my disability, I needed to look at doing something indoors, in airconditioning, maybe something with a computer. But there was no way I could come at that. All I'd ever wanted to be was a farmer. Anyway in the short term, I had no choice. I had no money, no livelihood, no one to look after me except my parents.

So on 5 January 1988 – when many Australians' attention was focussed on the approaching Bicentenary and fun and celebrations – I was discharged from the spinal unit.

My departure was much earlier than expected. Initially the doctors had told us that someone with my level of injury could expect to be in the spinal unit for about nine months. But after little more than five months they felt there was nothing more they could teach me. It was time to make it on my own.

It was a farewell of mixed feelings. As my parents and I said goodbye to some of the staff at the entrance to the unit, it was like parting with family members after so many months in their care. Among them was my doctor, Dr Bill Davies. He said, 'Well Sam, I'll give you one bit of advice. Take risks.'

He hardly needed to say it really. I'd been a risk-taker all my life, no doubt the reason why I was so accident-prone.

We climbed into the car and headed home, with me in the front passenger seat because it was most accessible, and my poor mother relegated to the back seat, as she was to be for the next twelve years whenever I was travelling with them. At the point when she and Dad were on their own for the first time virtually since they married, their privacy was all about to end again.

And so I came home, as I had always planned. But instead of me walking, my dad pushed my wheelchair fifty metres across the homestead lawn and up two timber planks into the gauzed verandah on the western side of the house.

As anticipated, the modifications weren't finished at home. The structure for my bedroom/bathroom had been built but the verandah floor was still dirt. There were no ramps to get inside my bedroom or the house, only planks of wood. After the comfort and accessibility of the spinal unit, it was terribly primitive and difficult. Inside my bedroom there was just a single bed, a bedside table and desk, magazines, pen and paper to write on. There was no floor covering or shelving; that came later.

In the adjoining bathroom, the plumbing was in place but the water wasn't hooked up. For the first few days we hung the end of a garden hose over the shower rose. The hose ran out through the door, across the lawn to a garden tap. When I was ready for my shower, I yelled out to Mum, 'Righto, you can turn it on.' She'd turn on the tap and cold bore water poured over me. I'd wet myself, lather myself with soap, wash it off with the hose, then yell out, 'Okay. You can turn it off now.'

Thank goodness it was summertime. But the hot weather brought its disadvantages too. The heat knocked me for six. There was no airconditioning in my bedroom or the main house for some weeks. The only cooling was from a borrowed electric water cooler in my bedroom and an evaporative airconditioner in the guest cottage, the building that contained my old bedroom.

It seemed that for days on end I had to be pushed across the lawn and pulled up the couple of steps into the cottage so I could sit in front of the airconditioning trying to get my body temperature down. It was pretty demoralising. Just through the wall was my old bedroom, with my footy boots that would never kick another football, my cricket bat that would never slog another six and my surfboard that would never crest another wave. Rugby games and cricket matches and family holidays on the beach were mere memories. My two-wheel motorbike sat waiting for me in the car shed, never to be ridden again.

Only now was I realising the enormity of what had happened

to me and its full consequences. This was the lowest point ever for me. It was hitting me in my face. I could reach out and feel my footy boots, touch my surfboard and see my motorbike in the shed. It really started to sink in.

And it was shattering because it wasn't how I expected my homecoming to be. Like anyone who has had a stint in hospital, I thought getting home was the ultimate. I assumed that my life would get back to some degree of normality pretty quickly and I'd done the hard yards in hospital.

I was dreadfully, horribly wrong. In reality it was much harder when I came home in those first few weeks and it dawned on me just how massive the mountain in front of me was. It was gigantic, like a Mount Kosciusko. My life was never going to return to how it was. I finally knew that then.

The total extent of my injury was also finally hitting me like a gale force wind. I had bladder infections and bowel accidents. There I was at twenty, having to get my mother to clean up after my bowels had unceremoniously emptied themselves in the middle of the night. Meanwhile, bladder infections frequently turned me into a sweating, throbbing heap. All I could do was take antibiotics and go to bed and try to sleep until the drugs kicked in and eased the aches and pains. Each bladder infection left me drained like an empty water bottle. I took days to recover.

I was home for only a week when a rash broke out across my stomach and arms. Gradually the rash turned into little infected sores and spread down my body. They got worse and worse until I had big puffy irritations all over my backside. My poor mother had to clean and dress these oozing, pussy sores that seemed to be in every crack and crevice. I was mortified and embarrassed, and so was she. I remember lying there one day, no doubt with a pained expression on my face as she cleaned the wounds and she said, 'Sam, you hate it and I hate it but I'm afraid we're stuck with it, boy.'

Finally we summoned an ambulance and I went to see my doctor, who took one look at me and admitted me to Warialda hospital with suspected scabies. A phone call to the spinal unit in Brisbane confirmed they'd had a case around the time I left and as it was highly contagious and generally contracted from a hospital, it was obvious that was where I'd caught it.

So on Australia Day, in the Bicentennial Year when people across the nation were celebrating two hundred years since the arrival of white man, I returned to hospital. Just when I felt like I was making some progress, by getting out of the spinal unit and back home, within three weeks I was back in hospital. And it was even worse because Warialda's small hospital wasn't set up to handle someone with spinal injuries. While the staff were wonderful and supportive, they had no idea about the special needs of quadriplegia.

I was so miserable Dad decided to do something to cheer me up. He went to the Warialda newsagency and asked for some scratchies.

'How many?' asked the newsagent.

'Just keep pulling and I'll tell you when to stop,' said Dad.

The surprised newsagent did as he was told. 'That'll do,' said Dad eventually and they wound up a roll of about twenty-five.

He arrived at the hospital with this huge spiral of lottery tickets and said, 'Here, Sam … this will keep you amused for a while.'

I scratched the lot and hardly won a thing, just a couple of dollars here and there. But would you believe that within a day or two, Warialda newsagency sold a scratchie worth $80,000 and the winner only bought one ticket.

A week later I came home. By this stage I had hot and cold running water in my shower, and I was able to wash by myself. I'd get into my bath chair, push myself under the shower and wet myself all over with a handheld shower rose. Then I'd clip it on the side of the chair while I soaped. Once I was clean, I'd wash the suds off, dry myself and climb back into bed.

On one particular night I didn't realise the hot water was still on – I must have bumped the tap. So while I was soaping myself, the hot water was running down the back of my leg. I didn't feel a thing. The following morning as I pulled on my sock, soft red blistered flesh came with it. I couldn't believe my eyes … what was it? I rolled my leg and discovered an ugly raw wound on the back. Off to the doctor I went again. I had a third-degree burn from the hot water running down my leg and it took months to heal.

I was starting to feel like a punching bag. My opponent was persistent, and wasn't going away – not ever. Each time when I thought I'd almost found my feet, I'd receive another blow.

Toileting myself was proving a massive challenge. For the first couple of weeks Bill slept in my bedroom with me to help me do catheters. I had to set my alarm to wake every four hours to empty my bladder. It was confronting for Bill. Suddenly, here was his big brother, his role model and sometimes guardian angel, reduced to a body on a bed and he had to help me pee. It was pretty tough for everyone.

I was wetting my bed at night almost constantly; as I wrestled with managing my bladder, bowel accidents were common occurrences. Some mornings, it was all too much and I couldn't bring myself to tell Mum I'd soiled the bed yet again. I'd leave her to find the mess. But to give her her due, she usually cleaned it up without a fuss and we both pretended it hadn't happened. That's how we coped.

To make things even worse, I couldn't do anything on the farm. All I'd do was get up in the morning and go and sit in the sun. Then when it got too hot, I'd sit in front of the airconditioner in the guest cottage loungeroom, with my old bedroom next door. The remnants of my old life were a mere wall away, and they were a whole world away. While I sat there, everyone else was busy with the everyday running of the farm. There were big semi-trailers and B-double trucks to be loaded with grain from our winter wheat crop, harvested a month or two earlier. There were paddocks to be worked up with a tractor and plough ready for the next crop, sheep to be jetted against fly strike and drenched to kill worms.

Occasionally I'd go for a drive around the property with Dad, but that was more torment than anything because I'd see something that needed doing and I couldn't do it. I'd see a gate that needed putting on its hinges or a fly-blown sheep that needed treating, a car that needed washing or a lawn that needed mowing. I couldn't do any of it.

My brother, Bill, was out in the paddock helping Dad. He said, 'I was thinking to myself, Sam must be going around the bend. He can't do anything … that was the really, really low point.'

There were several times in those early weeks when I wondered if perhaps an office job and a computer and a move to a bigger centre might have been the way to go, like the spinal unit staff had suggested. But I didn't want to give up my dream and for the short term, I had no choice. I had nowhere else to go. I had no money, no job and couldn't take care of myself. I'd already given up so much, I couldn't bear to give up any more.

Despite the frustrations, I never really went through a period when I was so unhappy I didn't want to come out of my room. There were times when I was pissed off but I kept that to myself. I suppose I used to get rid of those feelings the next day by getting up and trying to achieve something new. That would extinguish the torment and frustration I'd felt the day before. It would override it and I'd be able to forget about it. The other thing that helped was the constant flow of letters, phone calls and visitors I had even after I got home.

During the first month or so at home, I was still learning how to perfect the simple things, like eating, toileting and clothing myself. I was pretty keen to get out of the tracksuits and sandshoes preferred by the spinal unit staff. I wanted to wear normal clothes like jeans, riding boots and a buttoned shirt but I had to learn to dress all over again. It was a whole different ball game. Pulling on tracksuit pants, with their stretchy fabric and elasticised waist, was pretty simple compared with pulling on jeans, which were heavier, stiffer and less malleable.

Once I got the jeans on, I had to learn how to do up the fly and top button. Getting on my shirt wasn't too bad, but again I was then faced with lots of buttons – challenging for someone whose hands don't work properly. But dressing in jeans and a shirt, the clothes I wore before my accident, was important to my self-esteem. It made me feel more normal.

After a few weeks I could get up by myself, pull on my jeans and put on my shirt but then someone had to do up all my buttons for me and roll up my right arm sleeve, because my left hand wasn't good enough. I couldn't wait to get back into my RM Williams elastic-sided boots but for love or money I couldn't pull them on. I tried and tried and tried.

So every morning I'd have to wait until someone came to help me finish dressing and pull on my boots. It was intensely frustrating. It was a big commitment for my family in those early few weeks. They even had to cut up my food.

At that stage, everyone in the family was probably wondering where this was all going to lead. There were no answers, no 'how to' or *Quadriplegia for Dummies* books. Nor did I know any other quadriplegics who were living on farms who could give me advice.

At night I was a little more independent. I could get undressed, have a shower and get back into bed by myself. Gradually I learnt to do more, often out of necessity and sheer frustration. Often at mealtimes, Mum would be on the phone and Dad would be outside working. My food would be sitting on the plate in front of me and I'd be starving. So I figured out how to cut up my own food, weaving my fork through the fingers of my virtually useless left hand.

One day, I was waiting for Mum to help pull on my boots and I became impatient. I decided to have another go at doing it myself. I slipped the boot opening over my toes, grabbing the tag at the back and pulling the boot towards my heel. As with when I'd tried previously, my leg and foot slipped left or right and I couldn't get the heel to slide into the boot, but I was burning with determination and eventually I managed to pull it on. I'd done it! What a sense of achievement.

I sat on the verandah of my bedroom and waited for Mum. She came out of the house apologising. 'Sorry, Sam, I got caught up on the phone ...'

I just sat there, smiling. 'Where are your boots?' she asked. Normally I had them sitting on my lap, ready for her to put on. I pointed towards my feet, my smile growing larger. It was a big moment for us both, a little blip of happiness at that very low point of my life.

The thing that kept my sanity was a Honda Odyssey – a four-wheeled buggy with a big bucket seat that sat low to the ground between the four wheels and had a roll cage over the top. It was powered by a 350cc motor and went like the clappers when it was flat out. Dad had obviously had a premonition that when I got home I wouldn't be able to do anything, so it was there when I arrived.

It was perfect for me. It was all hand controlled and needed no modification at all. While I had to be lifted in and out, because it was impossible for me to do it by myself, once I was strapped into the safety harness, I felt in control and secure. The seat was really comfortable, too. But the novelty quickly wore off because I'd come home from a ride and not be able to find Mum and Dad to help me out or I'd want to go for a ride and it would be the same.

Then one day I decided to try getting in myself. I pushed my chair up beside the Odyssey, with the right front corner facing slightly inwards. The distance between the seat of my wheelchair and the bucket seat in the Odyssey yawned like a chasm, more than half a metre across and half that down. Initially, I had to swing my body across about thirty centimetres onto the roll bar at the side, then in the second transfer, across and down a similar distance into the seat. While I was doing that, I also had to push my legs across. I started by lifting my right foot onto the seat, then my left. I placed one hand on the roll bar of the Odyssey, another on the seat of my chair and lifted my body across. I went crashing onto the ground.

In fact, I ended up on the ground three or four times. Invariably, when I fell it was because I lost my balance because that was – and remains – my biggest daily challenge. The ongoing task of trying to stabilise my entire body with two part arms and only one good hand took just about everything I had. Often I'd lose my grip and end up head over turkey or out the back of my chair.

With practice, I've learnt to understand in detail how my body moves. Like stacking a house of cards, it takes only one thing out of place to bring it all tumbling in a heap. And like with cards, I can't feel if I'm in balance – it has to be done visually.

After I fell while trying to climb into the Odyssey, I began the painstaking task of starting again. First, I managed to get myself in between my chair and the buggy. I tried to lift myself back onto the chair. I couldn't lift that high. Then I realised it was easier if I took away the cushion, making the seat lower.

Once back in my chair, I wheeled over to a nearby car, transferred into the front seat, put my cushion back in place, and returned to my wheelchair. Then I tried getting into the Odyssey again. The first time took ages but once I got my legs in and I managed to sit my backside on the rail of the rollbar I was right. I pushed my legs in a bit further and collapsed into the bucket seat. At last I'd made it.

When I drove away that day I went a little faster than normal – my spirits soaring. I tore down the road, dust billowing in my wake and grinning from ear to ear. What a feeling!

Getting out was the reverse of getting in but it was an even bigger task. Using my arms, I had to lift eighty kilograms of dead weight straight up thirty centimetres. A couple of times I fell back into the seat and started to wonder if I might have to wait for Mum or Dad to help me out. But I kept trying and in the end I succeeded.

Mum tells the story of being on the phone and hearing the Odyssey drive off and thinking it must have been Dad. She walked outside and saw my empty wheelchair sitting in the garage. When I returned, her smile was probably three times bigger than mine.

A few weeks later she wasn't quite so happy. I was driving the Odyssey down the airstrip near the house when I took a sharp turn to the left, planning to duck over the front ramp into the garden. I wasn't going all that fast, but both right-hand wheels dug in and the momentum was enough to throw the buggy completely over onto the roof and roll bars.

Thank goodness for that strong steel frame and the safety harness. I hung there suspended, with my heart pounding. But I was okay. I released the clips on the seatbelt and crashed onto the ground, dragged myself out of the roll cage and propped myself up against the side.

Fortunately I was within yelling distance of the house and in no time Mum and Dad came running. Their first glimpse of the upside-down Odyssey and the sound of me yelling must have just about given them a heart attack, but they quickly discovered I was all right. Together they were able to roll the buggy back onto its wheels and help me back in. Away I went as if nothing had happened, while my parents said later, 'As if we hadn't already been through enough.'

Aside from that one mishap, the Odyssey gave me something very important. It allowed me to get out of the wheelchair and gave me some freedom. But it wasn't perfect. It was too low to the ground to open or shut gates or go across the paddock. It didn't have the room to take my dogs or carry a passenger, and I used to come home covered in grass seeds and dust and almost deaf from the sound of the engine. I still needed to find something more versatile. But what?

Being paralysed from the chest down, I thought I was going to have to find something with a big bucket seat to support my trunk. And I couldn't rely on strength to help because with only two part arms and one hand, I didn't have any.

In effect, I was exploring uncharted country. As I mentioned before, I didn't know of any other quadriplegics living and working on farms. There were some paraplegics, but they were a whole different kettle of fish to me because they had their upper body power and strength. They could lift and heave and pull and shove. But I had to find another way to function on the land. All I could do was push down and lift. Nonetheless getting in and out of the Odyssey amazed everyone, especially at the spinal unit. And it inspired me to dream of other possibilities, beginning a chain of events that changed my life forever.

SEVEN

FINDING MY LEGS

Perhaps one of the biggest lessons I've learnt in life is to never give up, to be willing to try anything and everything, even if it seems impossible. If I'd dismissed things that I thought I couldn't do, I'd probably still be sitting in the house all day, in front of the airconditioner, watching television and desperately down and out.

That lesson was driven home to me more than a year after my accident when Dad came home from Moree with a four-wheel motorbike on the back of his Toyota trayback. He'd taken our two-wheel bike in for a service at the local motorbike dealership in Moree and the owner suggested he bring home the four-wheeler for me to try.

Four-wheel bikes, or all terrain vehicles (ATVs), were only just becoming popular on farms at the time. I'd considered trying one earlier but then rejected it. The biggest problem was they had no back support. For the life of me, I couldn't see how I'd be able to keep my balance, let alone operate the throttle or brakes on the handlebars. The foot-operated gears seemed completely beyond me.

While the owner of the bike shop had been very generous offering Dad the second-hand bike to take home for me to try, I'm sure he didn't realise, like most people, that I had no trunk muscles and my hands didn't work properly. But Dad didn't like to knock back such a kind offer. I remember him getting home and explaining what had happened. Dad said, 'I didn't like to say to the bloke, you don't really understand, Sam won't be able to use it …' He thought it was easier just to take it home and when he was going back into town the next week, he'd take it back.

A day or two later I headed across the lawn to the shed to get into the Odyssey. The four-wheel bike sat there taunting me with endless possibilities – 'if only' I could have ridden it. I looked at it, like a kid looking at a lollipop just out of his reach. Then I thought, 'Why not have a go at getting on?'

I wheeled up beside the back tyre. The mudguard and seat were about fifteen to twenty centimetres above the height of the cushion on my wheelchair and it was almost half a metre across to the seat. It was an enormous distance to lift almost 80 kilos of mostly dead weight.

I'm sure if any of the therapists in the spinal unit had seen me sidle up to the bike that day, they would have wondered how I was ever going to get up there. The first couple of times I failed dramatically, ending up on the concrete floor. But like the first time I got into the Odyssey, I managed to get myself back up into my chair and start again. I gave it everything I had and finally I got my bum up and across onto the seat.

There I was with my bum on the seat and my upper body leaning forward over my wheelchair like a top-heavy, precariously balanced pile of hay bales about to topple any moment. But I was determined not to end up on the ground again, and gave myself an almighty push.

It must have been a hilarious sight as I lurched and shoved my unco-operative body into an upright position. I was trying to stop myself from falling forward but also didn't want to push too hard or I'd go right over the other side. I definitely didn't want to do that, because then I'd have to drag myself on my backside all the way around the bike to get back into my wheelchair. At one stage I thought, 'Sam, what in the bloody hell are you doing this for?'

Finally my persistence paid off. I was upright. Then I looked down and realised what a long way it was to the ground!

But an amazing thing happened. I grabbed the handlebars with my right hand and then my left and felt incredibly stable and safe. I could control my trunk and hang on. My arms gave me leverage. I couldn't believe it. I was sitting on the bike!

Even so, I couldn't celebrate just yet. I still had both my legs on one side of the seat. I had to work out how to manoeuvre my right leg over the fuel tank to the other side. I took my right hand off the handlebar and almost fell off. I fought to keep my balance and finally managed to pick up my right leg and throw it over the bike. Once I'd done that it really gave me some stability.

Then I thought, 'Well, you've got this far, you might as well go for a ride.' I started up the bike and pulled the reverse lever, which was within easy reach, unlike the forward gears. I backed it gingerly out of the shed. Simple.

Now how was I going to get the bike into first gear? Obviously I couldn't use my foot. Clinging on for dear life, I managed to lean forward and pull the lever near my foot, then straightened and slowly accelerated. I puttered around the shed, then headed down the track a bit, the wind in my face, with a huge smile. It was like driving a car for the first time, catching my first fish, shooting my first rifle all rolled into one. I was elated, euphoric – like a kid at his first Christmas.

I simply couldn't believe the control and balance I had. It was so easy to operate. To think I might not have even tried it! That thought often goes through my mind, even today when I just whiz out to the shed, jump on my bike without giving it a thought and hoon off at a million miles an hour. The experience taught me that you've got to have a go at everything, especially when you're disabled.

It won't always work. After my accident I desperately wanted to get back on a horse and while I was still at the spinal unit we found a disabled riding school. I had to be lifted onto the horse and when I was up in the saddle I needed to be supported by people on both sides. I couldn't even feel the horse under me. If I'd shut my eyes I wouldn't have known whether I was on a horse or sitting in a chair. It was no fun at all but at least I tried. That was the important thing and once I knew it wasn't enjoyable, I was fine with that.

Discovering the four-wheel bike opened a whole new world for me. Until then my only form of mobility around the farm had been the Odyssey, with all its limitations. But the bike threw the gates of possibility wide open and my life fell into a new pattern. I'd get up in the morning, down breakfast, grab my dogs, get on the bike and head out into the paddock. There was nowhere on the farm I couldn't go. Suddenly I could open and shut gates, ride through the creek and up and down gullies and hills. I could take my dogs with me on the back or carry small items or another person.

We were farming a couple of thousand acres at that stage and I helped ferry people and machinery about. I installed a two-way radio on my bike and could come whenever anyone called for help. I soon put a spray rig on the back of it and a slasher on the front, so I could spray weeds and slash around the sheds and yards. I could pull up beside a water pump and start it. I could go down to the mailbox and collect the mail. Suddenly I had so many options.

In the late 1980s we ran only sheep on Bardin. Now I could muster them to the sheepyards – a job I often did all by myself. Once they were shorn, drenched or jetted, I could take them back to the paddock. I did try helping Dad draft them one day. I remember pushing my wheelchair through the sheepyards to the drafting gate and within seconds I was covered in sheep shit. It picked up on my wheels, which then scraped onto my clothes and came off all over my hands. Little bits of sheep manure flicked up everywhere. I was like a lamington rolled in green coconut – flecks of manure everywhere. That was my first and last attempt at helping in the yards. But again, at least I gave it a go. I had to be content with knowing I'd done a fair job getting the stock to the yards in the first place.

Best of all, I felt useful and part of a team. Before that, unable to help out in any way, I'd felt like a freeloader. At twenty years of age it was terrible. And deep down a nagging question had always tormented me. Were the staff at the spinal unit right after all? Was it possible for a quadriplegic to be a farmer? There were nights I lay in bed and thought perhaps it would be easier to move to a bigger city and get an office job, one where I wouldn't have to cope with extremes of isolation and temperature. The bike squashed those thoughts completely. Mastering it was a turning point, the moment when I knew I'd made the right decision about coming home, that there was a place for me back in the bush. I'd found my legs and finally knew once and for all that a quadriplegic could be a farmer.

While things were starting to happen for me on the farm, my social life still had a long way to go. My biggest frustration was not having my own transport. I was a few kilometres from my closest neighbours and sixty kilometres from my nearest town, so if I wanted to see anyone apart from my family and workmen on the place, I had to travel. That meant relying on family or friends, and with the big distances it was a huge ask. Not only did people have to give me a lift to my destination, they had to have an airconditioned vehicle with room for a wheelchair. They also had to lift my chair in and out and load and unload my luggage. Often I turned down invitations because the whole thing was such a hassle.

The only solution was to get some wheels of my own. So a few months after getting home, I ordered a new vehicle – a bright red Ford ute. I was incredibly excited, only to find out there were no red utes available and I'd have to wait a few months to get one. Would I like a sky blue one instead? No, definitely not. I'd wait for my red one.

The day I collected it I was like a dog just let off the chain. Dad and I picked it up at the local dealership and Dad had to drive it home because I didn't yet have my special licence. I couldn't wait to drive it myself and Dad had no sooner got out before I was behind the wheel. I spent hours driving around the farm, up and down the airstrip and our farm tracks, getting used to the hand controls. This was a mechanism that attached underneath the steering column – with two rods, one to the brake and the other to the accelerator. A handle projected at right angles underneath the blinker control. I pushed forward on the handle to brake and down to accelerate.

I had to train myself to automatically push my hand forward to put on the brake instead of pushing my foot to the ground in case of an emergency. I practised that over and over again. I also had to learn to work the blinkers and windscreen wipers with my left hand, while it still held the steering wheel because my right hand was needed on the hand controls. Meanwhile, I had to maintain my balance – particularly when going around corners.

That was seriously reinforced on my first trip to Moree with Mum. As we approached the main street, she was getting a bit jittery. 'Sam, we might avoid all this traffic and shoot around the back way,' she suggested.

I immediately put on my blinker, made a right turn and fell sideways into her lap. We started heading towards the footpath, where an old lady was steadily pushing her shopping trolley. Luckily, Mum's reflexes were quick. She heaved me back upright and I was able to make the correction but I don't think the old lady thought it was very amusing. I imagine she probably saw her whole life flash in front of her in those few seconds.

Not long after my encounter with the granny in Moree, I was driving home from Croppa Creek one night in the middle of winter. I reached over to grab something on the passenger's seat and lost my balance, and my head and shoulders fell across the console. Before I could push myself back up, the ute bolted off the road, careered down through a culvert and straight through a three-strand barbed wire fence. Luckily the bullbar caught all three wires and they snapped before I came to a halt in a stubble paddock.

With a fair bit of effort, I was able to straighten myself, to discover my bullbar a little the worst for wear. It sat at a precarious slant and I thought, 'Bugger, I've done a tyre.' With visions of having to endure a long and chilly night waiting for dawn and the earliest possible rescue, I tried out the ute. I went forward and back, right and left and discovered the tyres were all right after all.

Now all I had to do was find my way back to the road and off home I'd go. I spun the car around to face the direction from which I'd come – or so I thought – and couldn't see any tyre tracks. I turned off my headlights, thinking I'd see the lights of Croppa Creek or a house I knew wasn't far up the road. It was only about 8pm – their lights should still be on. Darkness, not a light to be seen anywhere. I drove around a bit more and came to a gully and thought, 'If you cross that, you'll really be losing your way.' I couldn't get my bearings at all. I've heard stories about people – especially itinerant workers who don't know the area – getting lost while driving machinery in a paddock at night. Some get off the tractor or header to go home and can't find their way out. I never thought it would happen to me!

Finally, as I spun the ute around yet again, the glint of a red reflector on a guidepost blinked at me. Thank God. Not letting the red reflector out of my sight, I headed straight for it. And you wouldn't believe it, I arrived at the fence in exactly the right place – a gaping hole and the broken wires welcomed me.

The next morning I had to go back down to Croppa Creek and all the way I was thinking I must ring the owner of the paddock – who I knew quite well – and tell him what happened. As I drove towards the spot where I'd had my little escapade, I spotted the landowner patching a bit of fence just a few hundred metres away from my entry and exit point. I pulled up, had a bit of a chat and finally raked up enough courage to say, 'I had a bit of a mishap on my way home last night. Actually I ran off the road and I went through your fence down there. If you go down a bit further, you'll find a bit of a gap.'

He couldn't stop laughing. He thought it was a great joke. And of course, the story flew around Croppa Creek in about five minutes. For months afterwards, whenever I was on my way home after a night out, everyone would sing out, 'Are you going to end up in Ando's paddock tonight, Sam?', 'Keep away from Ando's paddock tonight, won't you,' or, 'Will we come looking for you in twenty minutes? We'll know where to start looking, anyway.'

With time and experience I learnt to brace myself before I turned my ute to the right and not to try to pick up things from the passenger's seat when in motion. It was indicative of the whole mind shift that was required after my accident – how I had to learn everything over again, even the simplest things.

A few weeks after I got my ute Dad and I drove to Yetman, a village northeast of our place, for my driving test with a young policeman there. I was very nervous, like a seventeen-year-old getting my licence for the first time all over again. I was wondering what he'd make me do and if I'd be able to handle it. But it was simple. I had to drive around the block, park, do a three-point turn and drive back to the police station to fill out the paperwork. Elated, I drove home with my new licence.

The ute made an enormous difference to my life. Now I was independent away from the farm. I could travel anywhere by myself under my own steam. I started accepting invitations again and my social life took off. I felt like other young country blokes once more, driving my red ute with its bullbar, a proper one this time, and spotlights. It brought me freedom and a sense of identity.

A year or two down the track, one thing continued to evade me. I really wanted to be more involved with the grain production on our farm. It was my passion and I dearly wanted to operate the machinery. My biggest obstacle was getting from ground level up into the cabin of the tractors, header, front-end loader or dozer.

I knew that once I was up in the driver's seat I'd be right. We proved that the first harvest after I came home when my brother, Bill, gave me a fireman's lift up the ladder into the header a couple of times. It was tough on him. He had a bad knee from a rugby injury and I was pretty heavy. But it was the emotional rather than physical challenge that he remembers. 'It was a huge reality check. When I got that close to Sam, picking him up and carrying him around, it brought home just how disabled he really was. It was much more confronting than sitting at a dinner table with him in a wheelchair having dinner. I don't think I ever really got used to that.'

During that summer of late 1988, I loved getting back into the header. It was one of the first times I forgot about the wheelchair and I drove the header for a few hours that day. But it was too hard physically for Bill to keep lifting me two to three metres up the steep, narrow stairs into the cabin. So I had to be content with helping on the ground. It was frustrating because I knew once I was up in the cabin, everything was made for me. I had airconditioning, a radio and was able to drive with no modifications. A simple adjustment to the steering column to move it closer to me and I was operative.

At night, I lay in bed trying to think of a way I could get up into the cabin. The biggest problem always was the fact I had such limited upper-body strength. I searched for information or ideas, but the only things I found were for paraplegics, amputees or others who were much stronger than me. I had to find another way.

We considered digging a hole in the ground and driving the machinery in or building a launching pad off the woolshed. The trouble was that each piece of machinery was a different height. I felt the solution lay in finding something that could lift me up into the cabins, maybe something with a seat attached. One day we tried using our jib crane, a long pole supported by stays and operated by the three-point linkage on a tractor. Like most cranes, it had a hook on the end and was used for lifting things. They were quite common on farms back then.

We put the jib on the back of a tractor, found an old iron plough seat and welded it onto the end. Then we welded an old bit of pipe on as an armrest for me to hang on to for support. But then we hit a snag because we couldn't keep the seat horizontal. When the crane was down at wheelchair level, I was practically sliding off. When it was right up, I almost tipped off the other way. To make things worse, with Dad controlling the up and down movement of the crane from his tractor it was difficult to communicate over the noise of the engine. He couldn't really see what was happening at my end.

But we gave it a try. We had about five goes at getting through the door of a tractor, and it took ages to get level with the seat so I could transfer. Up and down we went, with me yelling instructions and the jib jerking all over the place. How I never fell off I'll never know, but I made it eventually.

It wasn't perfect but it was a start. I could see the jib wasn't going to work – it was inefficient, couldn't stay permanently on the tractor and wouldn't always be around when I wanted to climb on or off machinery. Yet again, I found myself thinking there was a solution out there – all I had to do was find it.

Finally, an idea came to me one day while I was driving down the main street of Moree. I was behind a ute with a small hoist attached to its tray. I thought, 'There's something I might be able to use.' It meant taking the idea with the jib crane a step further, if I could only figure out how to keep the seat level, no matter how high or low the hoist was.

I bought a hoist, which was like a mini crane, and we bolted it onto the tray of our old Toyota Hilux. It sat there for quite a while and we often used to play with it. It had a hand control, which meant I would be able to move myself up and down, a major improvement on the jib. The biggest challenge remained the seat – attaching it and keeping it level.

One day we had a half-handy bush mechanic came out to our place repairing machinery. I showed him the hoist and explained the problem. Next time I saw him he said he had an idea so we took it into his workshop in Warialda and left it. Three days later, he rang to say it was ready. He'd taken a plastic kitchen chair seat and mounted it on the end of the hoist, then designed a see-saw arrangement that kept it level. He'd tried it out with practically everyone who walked into his shop – light blokes, heavy blokes and everyone in between. Up and down, up and down. He was terribly excited about it.

We brought it home and put it to the test. Dad backed up the Hilux to the header. I drove my bike alongside the hoist and transferred into the seat. Using the hoist's hand controls, I raised myself up, and Dad drove my bike away from under me. He then slowly backed the Hilux while I adjusted the hoist up and down until the height was right for me to go through the cabin door.

Once inside, I lined myself up with the header seat and threw myself across. Then Dad drove the Hilux away. I was finally in the header and knew my new hoist would work for all the other machinery as well. A few minor modifications and I was away. Both tractors needed hand clutches. The loader was hydrostatic but the throttle was activated by foot. To get around that we welded a bit of pipe down to the accelerator so I could move it by hand. The turning brakes on the dozer were also on the floor, so we devised a wire rope that went around a number of pulleys, linking the brake and clutch. That way, when I pulled on the clutch, I also pulled on the brake.

Over three or four months, with help from our bush mechanic, we modified everything. In the end, I reckoned I could get on the machinery nearly as quickly as anyone else. I still wasn't completely independent – I was happy for someone to check the oil, water and fuel; it made everything a lot easier. But the hoist took all the work out of getting me into and out of the machinery.

What I realised was that simplicity is the key. We tend to look for complicated solutions to problems when often there's a simple answer.

The hoist made an incredible difference to my life. All of a sudden I could drive a header at harvest time and play a part in the preparation of crops. I could get on the dozer and push and pull or get on the front-end loader and lift and heave.

I think the greatest thing was knowing that I was now making a serious contribution on the place. As I've said, I wasn't entirely independent. Someone still had to be about to help in case something went wrong. If a bolt came loose on the header or a log got caught in the trash worker or something like that, I couldn't get off and fix it.

I hated having to call someone on the two-way knowing they'd have to leave whatever they were doing to come and help. Unfortunately, that was just the way it was – I had to accept that.

The only other worry was fire. Our summer harvest was often conducted in 40-degree-Celsius heat and a machine working in a dusty, dry crop was at risk of catching fire. Plenty of headers have gone up in smoke over the years. I'd given the fire danger some thought and I figured if the header did catch alight I'd open the cabin door, lower myself down as much as possible and throw myself onto the ground. Once I was on the ground, I could push along on my backside pretty well. Luckily, in eighteen years of harvesting I've never had a fire, although late one afternoon Dad took over from me and literally within minutes flames ignited behind the engine. He had to grab the fire extinguisher to put them out.

While obviously working with crops was my real passion, I continued to help with the livestock. A few years after I returned home, we bought a property next door that lent itself more to cattle than to sheep, so we gradually phased out the wool enterprise. It ended up being a smart business move because wool prices took a tumble in 1991 following abolition of the reserve price scheme and they've never fully recovered.

Selling the sheep certainly got rid of quite a bit of frustration for me. Personally, sheep required a lot more physical work, like jetting, drenching, shearing and crutching – things I couldn't do. Cattle were a different story. I could move cattle from paddock to paddock, check water and fences and start pumps. And with a fax, phone and agent, I could also do the marketing.

I became more absorbed with the cattle and because we were running a lot less – 300 cows as opposed to 3000 sheep – I got to know their characters as I rode among them most days. It was far more enjoyable. It had taken more than a decade in all, but I'd made it. My dream had finally come true. I was a farmer.

Along the way, there were quite a few mishaps and challenges. My first four-wheel motorbike came with a simple foot peg with nothing to hold my feet in place. They would often fall off and because I had no feeling, I was oblivious. I learnt to constantly glance at my feet to make sure they were still in place, but if I was chasing a sheep I'd be too busy concentrating on catching it and staying on the bike to notice where my feet were.

On a couple of occasions they came off the peg, were whacked on a log or rock or something, and I broke my ankle. I didn't get the instant sharp pain that other people did when I was injured. So I made the injury worse when I pulled my leg back on the foot peg, thought nothing of it and kept going. A few hours later I'd get a pounding headache and I'd suspect something was wrong. Then when I took my boot off that night to have a shower, I'd discover my ankle was the size of a pregnant elephant and I'd know I'd done some damage. There'd be another trip to the doctor, x-rays and I'd find my ankle was broken. The doctor would bandage my foot and ankle into a back slab and I'd have to keep it elevated for four to six weeks.

I soon worked out that I needed full footplates on the bike, all the way from the front mudguard to the back, with a lip on the outer edge as well, so my feet couldn't fall off. My life has been full of lessons and unfortunately I always seemed to have to fall into a hole before I learnt. It took two broken ankles before I designed myself safer footplates but I haven't broken an ankle since.

I've broken a few other things, though. One day I was mustering with Dad when some cattle broke away from the main mob and I took off after them, trying to turn the lead cattle back. I was flying along when I hit something in the long grass and the bike and I became airborne. I don't remember hitting the ground. I might have been knocked out for a while. Dad lifted me into the Toyota by wrapping his arms around my chest. I was only semi-conscious. He took me back to the house, and Mum asked me to count to ten.

'Two ... seven ... nine ... three ...'

Then I looked up and smiled at her. We all had a good laugh.

I lay down to rest and thought I'd be all right, but the next day my head was pounding. Again, I was off to the doctor, then x-rays. The radiologist said, 'You're a bit lucky, anyone else with five broken ribs would be in total agony.'

On another occasion Dad and I were mustering a mob of sheep. He was rounding up one side of the paddock and I was doing the other. I rode up onto a dam wall and noticed a lamb with its front legs bogged in the mud. Dad was way up the other side of the paddock, so I tried pulling it out by myself. It was on a fairly steep slope and I remember thinking, 'You'd better be careful you don't fall.'

I thought that if I could hook one arm around the handlebars of the bike and the other around the lamb's neck, with a bit of a pull I stood a pretty good chance of getting it out. I rode around the side of the bank, a little above the water in the dam. Just above the waterline there was a ring of mud where the stock were constantly putting their feet while drinking. That's where the lamb's front legs were stuck.

I parked the bike beside the lamb and things went according to plan until I tried to heave it free. My backside slid sideways off the seat of the bike towards the sheep. I still had one arm around the handlebars but I knew I was losing it and thought, 'Gees, you'd better hang on here because if you fall off, you'll go head first into the water.' I let go of the sheep and managed to grab my two-way radio mike. I tried calling Dad. No reply. As usual he had it turned down.

I knew I was in big trouble. Desperate, I called Mum, who was at home with Kate in the garden.

'Get to the Dunollie Hill dam … quickly!' I shouted.

'What's happened?'

'Never mind what's happened, just get here. It's a matter of life or death!'

Mum and Kate raced to the Toyota without even putting on their shoes. Kate got behind the wheel, while Mum climbed into the passenger seat and grabbed the two-way.

'We're coming through the first gate now, Sam. Are you there Sam?'

No reply.

'We're coming through the cultivation now, Sam. Do you read us?'

Still no reply.

'We're crossing the creek now, Sam.'

Silence.

When they got to the Dunollie Hill paddock gate, my dogs greeted them. By then, Mum and Kate didn't know what to expect. They hadn't heard from me for almost ten minutes.

They bounced their way as fast as they could across the paddock to the dam, to find me holding on for dear life. My left arm was still wrapped around the left handlebar. I'd long since dropped the mike of the two-way and was using my right hand to hang onto the rifle rack on top of the handlebars.

My bum had slipped right off the seat and wasn't far from the water. My left leg was sliding over the seat and fuel tank. My arms were killing me but I hung on because I was terrified that if I fell in, I wouldn't have been able to get my head out of the water. It's amazing how much strength and stamina you can muster when it's a life-threatening situation.

As Mum and Kate rushed to help, my sister, with her usual sisterly love and ironic sense of humour said, 'What the hell do you think you're doing?' They got below me, heaved me back up

124

onto the bike and then pushed it out of the mud. I revved it up and drove off without a word.

I was so pissed off. The whole time I had been hanging on for dear life, I could hear Dad's Toyota not far away. If he'd had his two-way turned up, I'd have had help in a few seconds and we'd have been finished mustering the paddock by now. Kate's voice followed me as I drove off, 'Thank you very much … thank you … thanks Mum … thanks Kate … jolly good of you to come over.'

I rode straight over to Dad and gave him a blast for not having his two-way turned up.

Mum says in hindsight, 'I have no doubt in my mind that Sam would have drowned if we hadn't heard the two-way because he couldn't have held on much longer. He probably wouldn't have been in much water, but it wouldn't have mattered. The scary thing is, we were out in the garden and it was a fluke that we heard the two-way.'

I was lucky, because nine times out of ten, the two-way in the house was also turned down because it was right beside the phone. Someone rings, the two-way is blaring and you turn it down thinking you'll turn it up when you get off the phone, but you never do. It was so bloody frustrating. But I could write a whole chapter on the things that happen with two-way radios on bush properties.

That and the challenges of staying on a motorbike when you're a quadriplegic. My problem was, being paralysed from the chest down and having no trunk muscles, it was hard to keep my balance and control the bike. The power of the machine alone was enough to throw me one way or another. Other people controlled their balance with their trunk muscles and gripped with their knees, hanging on with their whole lower body. I couldn't do that. So when I went around a corner or along a slope, I'd be trying to hang on, keep my balance and control the bike at the same time. Sometimes I slid off while doing something as simple as going around the side of a gully or over a contour bank. I'd be hanging on with my hands but my backside would be sliding off the seat. After a while I got to know my limitations but sometimes I'd miscalculate.

It goes without saying that I pushed things to the limit. Like the time I was riding along the creek bank, lost my balance and slid off the side. The bike then took off about fifteen metres down a steep slope, stopping at the bottom of the gully. It was still on its wheels with the engine idling. 'Bugger,' I said to myself. There I was, at the top of the creek bank with my bike at the bottom. My only lifeline, the two-way, was on the bike.

Nobody was going to come looking for me in a hurry and I was in a pretty isolated part of the creek, where no one would have expected me to be. So I figured I had to get out of this pickle myself. Bit by bit I gently manoeuvered myself down the slope, through the long grass and weeds towards my bike until eventually I got to the bottom. Then I had to get back on the bike.

It was a skill I perfected over the years. I'd sit with my back to the side of the bike then heave my backside up onto the foot peg. Then I'd lift myself up onto the seat. The first time I got back onto the bike, I took a whole lot of skin off my rear with the serrated foot peg. I didn't realise at the time, but that night when I got undressed there was blood everywhere and I discovered the damage. After that, any time I came off, I would take off my shirt and put it over the foot peg to protect my backside.

The other thing I had to be careful of was heat. One side of the bike was particularly hot because of the muffler. When I climbed on that side I had to be careful not to burn myself in the process. I did that once too.

Experiences like these reminded me how incapacitated I was. I'd fall off my bike or even out of my chair and be lying there and feeling completely helpless. Just sitting up was a struggle, let alone getting back into my chair, and the bike was even harder again.

One day I said to Mum, 'I wish I could get a chainsaw and cut all this crap off that doesn't work. It would make life so much easier because it's just dead weight that I have to lift.' Every day from the time I opened my eyes in the morning until I closed them at night I fought to keep my balance. It was – and is – my one most constant challenge. But that's the way it is and I just have to get on with it.

Despite landing myself in some pretty precarious situations over the years, I've always managed to get myself out of them, or help has been within reach.

Fencing wire has almost been my undoing on a number of occasions. It's one of my worst enemies. All it takes is a small piece of old wire in the grass to bring my bike to a grinding halt. Generally I've been able to lean over the side or back of the bike and cut it away but there have been times when it has been like a spider's web, impossible to remove. Then I've had to radio for help.

I knew my safety was always a worry for my parents and even when they were on holidays, I suspect a part of them never fully relaxed, wondering if I was all right. When they went away, they'd ask me to stay off the bike and the mower and anything else that could possibly break down, get a flat tyre or land me in trouble. Although I'd nod and say, 'Yes, I will,' before their dust had settled, I'd be on my bike and heading off somewhere, thinking innocently, 'I'll be very careful.'

But then I'd see a rogue cow in the crop and I'd think, 'I can't leave it there until Dad gets back,' so away I'd go after it, hit a bump and off I'd fly. Not that I was totally isolated. I always had the two-way and I could call a neighbour as a last resort. Like the day I rolled my bike in the creek. I was going down quite a steep gully at the time. Rather than going straight down, I was trying to go off to the side slightly. The further I went down, the more I lost my balance. Finally, I could feel myself falling off the bike, pulling it over with me. It rolled over twice before landing in the bottom of the gully with its four wheels in the air. It eventually flooded and stopped running. There was no way I could have got it back onto its wheels.

I gingerly slid on my backside down to the bike and grabbed the two-way – which by some miracle hadn't been damaged, thanks to the rifle rack on top of the handlebars, which took the brunt of the tumble. I called Jamie Donaldson and he came to my rescue. Jamie, or 'Dono' as we called him, was with me that day I stacked my pushbike on the way home from school all those years ago. He knew about my various other mishaps too, so he wasn't at all surprised to get my SOS, I'm sure.

I was lucky that day. My two-way was still in one piece and Dono was within range. I reckon if you sat down with any bloke in the bush who rides a four-wheel bike, they could probably tell you a humdinger story about their mishaps and how they survived. Of course, some don't live to tell the tale because those vehicles are involved in many deaths on Australian farms.

But most of us survive and get back on, and don't say anything to anyone about it. The last thing you'd go home and tell your wife was that you nearly killed yourself rolling the motorbike. If you did, she'd probably take the keys and throw them into a dam. As I said earlier my spinal unit doctor, Dr Davies, told me to take risks. So I did. Mind you, I didn't really need to be encouraged. I always have and I always will have a go. Life's too short to wrap yourself in cotton wool.

EIGHT

CLIMBING KOSCIUSKO

Since I was a child I have been captivated by things that fly, from the tiny willy wagtail to the huge wedge-tailed eagle, from a small crop-duster plane to a massive Boeing 747. Whenever a plane passed overhead I'd watch, engrossed, as it blazed a trail across the sky.

Perhaps that fascination began the day my uncle, Ian McGregor, flew Dad, Jamie Donaldson and me to Ag-quip, an agricultural field day at Gunnedah, about three hours' drive southwest of home. I was in fourth or fifth class at the time. I was so excited about the flight that I remember it better than the field day itself, despite the fact that it was one of the largest in the southern hemisphere.

Another time when I was still in primary school, there was a pig shoot in the district, using a helicopter. Dad was the navigator on one of the shoots and I went up with him. I sat between him and the helicopter pilot and was dumbfounded, blown away by the experience. I couldn't wait to climb in. Actually I think I was the first one in and last one out.

For me, flying was the ultimate experience. As the power of the plane or helicopter engine throbbed around me, it seemed to permeate my skin and seep into my very soul. I felt the power, the energy. At that moment when we left the ground, the sense of being airborne gave me a huge rush. I felt free, like an open-ended question of endless possibilities.

And then to be able to see forever into the distance, until it literally disappeared from view to my naked eye. I loved the space, the different perspective, the way the landscape turned into a roadmap – and I could see how the jigsaw of tracks and thoroughfares and properties all fitted. And kangaroos, pigs and livestock – as small as ants – brought tiny dots of movement to it all.

I was hooked. Just two flights and I was addicted for life.

Once I left school and headed north, I grew even keener. In outback Queensland and the Northern Territory, aeroplanes and particularly helicopters were used extensively for mustering. That whetted my appetite even more. When we were mustering at Avon Downs I was on horseback in the middle of 40-degree heat, sweating like a pig, and I looked up at this guy in a helicopter and thought, 'I'd love to swap him places.'

Sometimes I think that if I'd made it to the Camooweal pub that afternoon in 1987, I would have pursued my pilot's licence and ended up in planes or even more likely helicopters – they were my favourite flying machines. Perhaps it's a bit of a 'boys and their toys' thing. Some blokes like fast cars, some like yachts and some, like me, want a helicopter.

Then I had my accident and the dream of flying was shattered. I was having enough trouble just dressing and feeding myself, let alone flying. But over the months following my homecoming, the interest was rekindled. I had a couple of mates who were pilots and at different times they took me up in their planes. As we taxied down our airstrip, the blood would start pumping. Those old feelings came back strong and fast.

I also read an article in *ParaQuad*, a magazine for people with spinal injuries, about a paraplegic in Melbourne who was flying. The modifications he'd made to his aeroplane looked as though they'd suffice for me too and his story drove me on to think that maybe flying was still a possibility after all.

I started talking to everyone I knew who could fly, or had an interest in flying, about the options. I encountered some who were enthusiastic, others who told me I couldn't do it. Those individuals spurred me on even more.

My sense was that physically it would be possible, but the big stumbling block was finding the money. The more I looked into it, the further it seemed out of my reach. I just didn't have the spare cash.

I also considered helicopters. A nearby neighbour, Max O'Neill, was a pilot and had a helicopter so I rang him for a chat. He didn't like to squash my enthusiasm, but told me I'd need some serious funds to realise that dream. He also said, 'You've got to be an octopus to fly a helicopter anyway.' So that idea immediately got knocked on the head.

But Max planted the seed of another one. He mentioned that he was also a member of an ultralight club in Warialda; maybe that was an option. An ultralight was a small kit-built aircraft that looked similar to a hang glider, only with a motor and couple of seats. Mum made a similar suggestion around the same time, to which I replied, 'Oh, I wouldn't fly one of those stupid things.'

Yet a week later, I'd reconsidered. 'What's that bloke's name in Warialda? The one with the ultralight,' I asked Mum.

'Bruce McMullen ... he's the science teacher at the high school.'

'I might get in touch with him,' I said.

Bruce remembers that phone call vividly and was immediately enthusiastic about the idea. He said he really wanted to take me for a fly, to give me the chance to experience what he called the 'third dimension'.

He was the senior instructor with the Warialda Ultralight Club and was a qualified General Aviation (GA) pilot as well. While at that stage I hadn't actually seen an ultralight, I suspected it would be a fairly basic machine so it was comforting to me to know Bruce was also qualified to fly planes. I thought that, surely if he was so highly trained, he wouldn't get into an ultralight if he didn't think it was safe. Next morning I headed into Warialda with Jamie Donaldson, whom I'd talked into joining me.

I'll never forget seeing the ultralight for the first time. Bruce opened the hangar door as I was getting out of the car. I gazed into the hangar, thunderstruck by this bit of kite material wrapped over a frame. It didn't look like much at all. The motor would have been flat out driving a lawn mower. Donno and I were speechless and Bruce must have seen my jaw drop and my face go very pale as I thought, 'You're not going to get me into that thing!'

But it was too late to pull out by then. We went over, said hello to Bruce and he started telling us both about the machine. It was a Quicksilver MX2, manufactured in America and put together in Australia. It was a two-axes aircraft, which meant it only had two controls – a rudder and elevator operated by a single joystick between the two seats. They sat between two wheels that supported an A-frame, along with a nosewheel at the front. It was completely open to the elements.

Amazingly, it needed no modification for me to fly it, if I decided to go ahead and learn. I could also get in easily. One strut was partially in the way, but otherwise it was more or less a clean transfer from the chair to the seat of the ultralight. It was lower than my chair, so it was an easier lift than my bike, for example.

In fact, the whole ultralight experience was almost eerie. The chances of having an ultralight club in my closest town only forty minutes away, with an aircraft that I could use immediately without modifications and a qualified instructor undaunted by teaching a quadriplegic to fly seemed almost too good to be true. It was as though it was all meant to be.

Bruce pushed the ultralight out of the hangar; I climbed in and fastened the lap-sash seatbelt. He started it up and we taxied down to the end of the airstrip. The thought of taking off in this flimsy thing was daunting that first time. Was I really about to go flying in something so insubstantial?

We turned around and Bruce said, 'Are you ready?'

'You bet!'

And away we went. I still recall as clear as day that moment as we left the ground and how I simply loved it. It was unbelievable, exhilarating. It was the closest thing to being a bird that I could imagine. There I was sitting in a padded seat, a couple of hundred metres above the ground, the wind in my face and nothing between me and the sky. I was hooked.

Donno's turn was after me, and he too came back with a smile from one ear to the other. We knew without even exchanging a word that we were going to learn to fly.

At that stage I think my family had mixed feelings about my new sport. Mum put it this way: 'We didn't mind the ultralight at all – you had to stop worrying about things. All we wanted was to see him happy, and I always said, if he came down in the ultralight, as long as he didn't have my best friend's child with him, I'd at least know he'd had a smile on his face five minutes before.'

On the other hand, Mum and Dad probably did worry about me. They admit now there were times when I was later getting home than they expected or the wind came up, when they anxiously waited to hear the engine, or see the tiny red speck in the distance. Luckily for me, at no time did they discourage me.

So for the next six or seven months we learnt to fly. The really great thing was doing it with Donno because it meant we went to lessons at the same time, studied theory together and shared the excitement. We'd talk about flying for hours.

While we didn't need to have a formal licence to fly an ultralight, Bruce – being a qualified GA pilot – took training very seriously and we had to do a set number of hours in the air, as well as passing practical and written exams. I'm glad of that because back then, anyone could buy an ultralight kit, build it, read a book and take to the air. It was hardly surprising that ultralight pilots crashed every once in a while because what was described in a book and what happened up in the air were very different.

For our part, Donno and I also took our training seriously and attended lessons once or twice a week. We quickly mastered taking off and the manoeuvres in the air but it took a lot longer to perfect our landings. All novice pilots find that. I'd come in too fast one time; the next time I'd come in too slow. Then once I'd achieved a decent landing in good weather, I'd strike a windy day and I'd have to start all over again. But like most things, one day it just came to me.

Finally I was nearing my first major goal, flying solo. That's a day burnt into the memory of every pilot – the day your instructor decides enough hours together have been clocked up and he hops out and tells you to do it by yourself. First we did a couple of circuits and Bruce told me to land, let him out and take off alone, do a five-hundred-foot circuit and land again. When I landed, he got out and put a bag full of sand into his seat, so the balance of the plane felt the same as it always had. Over time we gradually removed sand until the bag was empty and I could fly alone, but that day it was full.

Bruce said later he felt going solo was my biggest achievement. Although he said he never heard a quiver in my voice as I prepared to fly by myself for the first time, I remember being quite nervous. He told me he was worried, not that I wouldn't be able to do it, but that I'd fail to meet my own high standards. 'Sam had demonstrated to me such a level of proficiency that anything but excellence wouldn't have been good enough for him ... he wasn't trying to impress me but he wanted to show me he could do it and that he could do it on his own.'

He was right – for me it was incredibly important to be able to prove I could do it by myself. It was about fighting for my independence. I suppose I was keenly aware that Donno was going to fly after me and I wanted to be on the same level as him, despite my disability. By then I'd had a taste of what it was like to achieve a small task for myself, such as doing up my first button or putting on my boots for the first time, and I wanted this to be the same, only many times multiplied.

I succeeded and so did Donno, and our solo flying began. For starters we did short trips, around the Warialda township, but after a while I felt ready to tackle flying home solo. To be honest, I felt a little daunted, worried about whether I'd be able to find my way, but I did find some familiar landmarks and then finally I recognised the white roof of Bardin house in the distance. I headed in that direction and Mum and Dad ran outside with a huge white sheet to make sure I saw them. I buzzed the house in glee … it was another exciting milestone.

Within a few weeks of going solo Donno and I passed all our exams and earnt our licences. Then, yet again, it seemed the flying was meant to be because the Warialda Ultralight Club decided to update their aircraft and offered to sell us the machine we'd learnt to fly in. We jumped at the offer and a few weeks later, after we'd built a hangar at the end of the Bardin airstrip, me and Donno flew it home.

It was an older plane and it required new fabric on its wings. When we began to sort that out, another eerie coincidence popped up; the distributor for the QuickSilver Ultralights lived at Yallaroi, about thirty-five kilometres up the road. He turned out to be a great bloke called Graham Steptoe, and Graham became an indispensable part of my flying maintenance. Without him I probably wouldn't have been able to fly as much as I did in a secondhand machine. In fact, he ended up spending so much time at Bardin that he became one of the family. He eventually built his own airstrip so I could fly to him for repairs and maintenance.

I practically spent my life in the ultralight once I brought it home. How I loved being up in the air with that wheelchair on the ground. The only restriction was to avoid the times when RAAF jets might have been flying through. We were under one of their Low Jet Routes (LJR) and I had to call the Amberley air base on weekdays to get the all clear, otherwise I would have been like a grasshopper hitting the windscreen of an F1-11.

With the hangar literally 150 metres from the house I could wheel down in my chair. Again, I needed someone to be there to fill it with fuel and push it out onto the airstrip but then I could do the pre-flight check, transfer into the seat, start the engine and take off all on my own. After I'd been flying I'd land, taxi back to my wheelchair, get out and go back to the house. If there was no one about, I could leave the ultralight and someone could put it away for me when it suited them.

I felt I'd conquered something amazing, climbed my very own personal Mount Kosciusko. Not in my wildest dreams did I ever imagine I would fly after I'd had my accident. Now I knew I could do anything. I remember telling my doctor back in Brisbane that I was flying an ultralight and he simply couldn't believe it.

Dad later shared his thoughts about it all: 'In a sense his flying was when he climbed the mountain. He proved nothing was impossible. It was the crowning achievement because suddenly he could do something that a lot of his friends couldn't do.'

Dad hit the nail on the head. When you're disabled you're dependent on a lot of other people to do various things for you. The flying gave me a sense of self and independence, largely because I'd acquired a skill that most other people didn't have. I was a pilot and I could do something for them by taking them for a fly.

In fact, I loved taking people up with me and took up more than 200 over the following few years. Most people would be on the phone before they came to visit, can we go for a fly, can we go for a fly? When they arrived, we'd go down to the hangar and they'd see this thing and go to jelly. They'd be shit-scared, just like me when I first saw it, but I've never had anyone refuse to go up.

Often it was a couple and the husband or wife would go first and come back with a smile wrapped around their face. Then the other one would climb straight in and they loved it too. They were big and small, old and young and very few got out and said, 'That was all right but I wouldn't do it again.' Most people said it was the best thing they'd ever done.

The person I enjoyed taking up most was my former house master at TAS, Jim Graham. He was coming to Bardin for a fundraiser we were hosting for the school to help raise money for an indoor swimming pool and I'd told him I was going to take him for a fly.

'That'll be terrific,' said Jungle but he told me later he was secretly hoping it would be too windy or raining. But it wasn't. It was a perfect day.

I could tell he was nervous from the moment he arrived and he slowly became quieter and quieter. I'd been down at the hangar with a mate and we'd fuelled, serviced and taken the machine for a quick spin. I didn't want any hiccups during this special flight.

After lunch and all the formalities, Jungle came down to the hangar and a crowd followed him. They lined up along the fence beside the airstrip. So there was Jungle, white and no doubt petrified, with a huge audience thrown in as well.

Later he said, 'Once or twice I thought this thing might crash … but then Sam's enthusiasm and joy at what he was doing transferred to me and I thought, if he crashed and killed us both, what did it matter?'

We taxied down the runway and prepared to take off.

'How are you feeling?' I asked.

'All right,' said Jungle.

'Well, I've waited and waited and waited to be in this position all my life and I can't believe that I'm here and you're there and you are just so bloody helpless. You are totally at my mercy,' I teased. 'And do you remember that time when I had that girlfriend out of town and you'd only let me go out to her place on weekends every now and then? I haven't forgotten that!'

Poor Jungle. But once we got up in the air, he relaxed. I did a couple of circuits and came into land, and could almost feel the relief radiating from the seat beside me. He didn't plead to go straight back up but I think he enjoyed it and he received a huge round of applause from the bystanders.

One of the most challenging things about flying an ultralight was its susceptibility to wind. Because it was so light, it was vulnerable to even the tiniest gusts. One day there was a bike rally from Warialda to Coolatai – about forty kilometres. I was a member of the State Emergency Service (SES) back then and local members were co-ordinating the ride. They asked me to fly to Warialda, pick up another SES member, then fly out with the cyclists – keeping an eye on the event from the air – and meet them at Coolatai.

We were a lot faster than the riders, and quickly overtook them. So I landed on the road about halfway out, waited for them to go past, then took off again and flew into Coolatai. I did a couple of joy-flights, but then the wind started to rise. As the gusts got stronger, I knew I had to get home – quickly.

I didn't have my wheelchair with me and that concerned me, so I said to the organisers, 'Look, I'd better pack up and get going because I think the weather's going to deteriorate.'

So I took off and headed for home and at one stage I felt I was going backwards, as I flew into the strong westerly. It was one of my most frightening flights, as the aircraft was tossed about like a leaf in a wind tunnel. Naturally, my parents were anxiously wondering where I was. I was very, very relieved to see our airstrip and I was even happier when I got my wheels back on the ground.

It was also windy the day I took one of my best mates from school, David Steffenson, for a ride. He was thinking, 'Beetle [my nickname from school] you buggered your neck, don't bugger mine!'

David described the experience like this: 'I remember sitting there, three or four hundred feet up, on a piece of aluminium and a plastic seat, flying over kangaroos and what not … then we had to try two or three times to land because there was a crosswind. We'd come down and Sam'd say, "No, we can't land this time, we're going to get flipped over …" And off we'd go again.'

All the while, his wife was standing on the ground watching. Obviously I was aware of the very precious cargo I had on board every time I took someone for a fly. In a sense it was an enormous responsibility because it was always someone's wife, husband, son or daughter, but I prided myself in getting them all back on the ground safely.

Dad, Bill and Kate were my most regular passengers. Dad always enjoyed it. He never had any desire to learn himself but loved nothing more than a circuit or two around Bardin. He helped me with my flying more than anyone, regularly filling the ultralight with fuel and pushing it out of the hangar, so often he'd jump in for a fly as well.

Kate was keen on the flying and went up at every opportunity; in fact we were constant companions during holidays when she was home from boarding school, getting up to all sorts of pranks and adventures. She never lost her enthusiasm for the sport. But it took a lot longer to talk Mum into joining me. I kept asking and asking, until one crystal clear, almost eerily still morning she finally agreed.

'I must admit there was something about it. It was like floating through the sky in an armchair. It was a bit scary when he banked to my side and I looked down and there was nothing ... but I came home feeling a million dollars about it,' she said later. She went up one other time. 'It was like having a baby. You swear you'll never have another one but then you front up again and when you start going into labour you think, "Oh my God, I remember what it's like now!"'

Bill, however, had slightly different memories of my flying. To begin with, he was almost as enthusiastic as I was. 'It was great fun, I really enjoyed it,' he said. He remembered some amazing flights, when we'd take off on an incredibly clear, still morning just as the sun was rising. He remembered flying three feet above the ground over crops, and wheat heads getting caught in the wheels of the ultralight. He remembered buzzing kangaroos and wild pigs from the air.

Then one night, when Bill was home from university, we decided to go flying the next morning. It was the middle of winter, and I said, 'Make sure you rug up because it'll be freezing.' As I was leaving my bedroom at daybreak I noticed a short red and white scarf and wrapped it around my neck, tucking it into my big coat tightly. 'That'll keep me a bit warmer,' I thought.

Down we went to the hangar, fuelled up the plane, gave it the usual pre-flight check and took off. We flew all the way down to the other side of Croppa Creek – more than twenty kilometres away by road – and we were on our way home, flying over the next-door neighbour's stubble paddock.

I'd given the joystick to Bill, which was quite difficult for him because he was sitting in the right-hand seat and had to use his left hand. We were flying along enjoying the view when all of a sudden, chug, chug, chug … the engine stopped!

There was an eerie silence. I didn't have to look back. Instantly I knew what had happened. The bloody scarf had come off, been sucked back into the propeller and stalled the motor. Bill looked over at me, his face the colour of arctic ice. He said later, 'I thought I was going to die.'

For a split second I panicked too, but then all my training for emergency landings automatically kicked in. I grabbed the stick and my instructor's words echoed in my head: 'Push the stick forward, keep up your air speed and select a spot to land.' And straightaway that happened; the training worked. I pushed the stick forwards and you wouldn't believe it, we were over this paddock and there was an airstrip in front of us. Although I suspected we didn't have enough height to reach it, the airstrip was in a cultivated paddock so I knew it didn't matter. We landed about fifteen metres from the runway. It was a textbook emergency landing.

When the ultralight came to a halt, we just sat there, our hearts pounding wildly. Then Bill spoke. 'Jesus, what happened?'

'The fucking scarf came off.' I looked back and, sure enough, the whole tail of the plane was covered in the red and white remains of my St George scarf.

Bill climbed out of his seat and slowly recomposed himself, then went to the back of the aircraft and pulled the mangled remains of the scarf out of the propeller in disgust.

When I said, 'Can you pull the plane over to the airstrip and we'll fly home?' Bill couldn't believe his ears.

'You've got to be joking!' he said. He was walking home. There was no way he was getting back into that thing.

But it was obvious he didn't have any choice. 'I realised that Sam couldn't walk home and I couldn't leave him there, so it was the only thing we could do. That made the whole thing worse, the fact I had to get back into the plane and fly home.'

While this was happening, Kate was on the garden lawn playing with our pet cocker spaniel. 'I watched the ultralight glide down below the treetops and didn't take any notice because Sam and I used to fly along the top of the wheat crop all the time. But then I was waiting for it to reappear and it didn't.'

She raced inside. 'Mum, Dad … Sam's plane has just come down.'

A few minutes later they were all standing in the garden, looking in the direction of where Kate last saw the ultralight, trying to decide what to do when they heard the engine, and up in the air went the ultralight.

As we were coming in to land – with Mum, Dad and Kate waiting near the hangar – I said, 'For Christ's sake, don't tell them what happened … they'll spew.' That was the final straw for Bill.

But of course the story did get out and my parents probably would have been quite happy to put a padlock on the hangar and never see the ultralight again.

Mum and Dad often used to joke when Bill and I went flying, 'Good God, we've got two of them up there now.' It didn't seem so funny any more, and I must admit Bill didn't go flying much after that.

He said, 'I just thought, what a silly way it would have been to go, if we'd both ended up dying because an old scarf got caught in the propeller. It was a real Biggles story.'

There was one passenger I was tempted to take up but never did. That was my black dog – a cattle dog, Labrador and dingo crossbreed called Dusty. Whenever I went to the hangar, Dusty followed and while I was flying, she waited by my wheelchair until I came home. After I'd landed and taxied back to the hangar she would often jump into the other seat and sit there, wagging her tail, delighted to see me. She was so pleased to see me that sometimes, as I taxied back down the runway, she'd run alongside and one day she even jumped in and rode with me while the aircraft was still moving. I really wanted to take her flying – she loved the motorbike and I thought she'd probably take to flying too – but I was never game, always afraid that she might bail out.

Despite the odd heartstopping moment in the air, to be able to fly away and get right away from that empty wheelchair was incredibly empowering for me. It symbolised leaving behind my disability in a sense, because in the air I was like anyone else. It was an enormous part of my psychological rehabilitation. It was about doing something that almost no one else could.

Most importantly, it showed me that anything was possible. Never again would I look at something and wonder whether I could do it. From then on I looked at things and thought, 'I'm going to do it. I've just got to think of a way of doing it.'

The flying was the greatest thing I'd done since my accident. And when I sat back and thought about it, I felt proud that, as a quadriplegic, I'd been able to achieve something like that.

There have been plenty of knockers along the way. People who told me I wouldn't be able to fly. They'd remind me that I was pretty incapacitated and I wouldn't be able to do it because of this or that. But that's life and human nature; some people will always tell you why you can't achieve things.

One bloke in particular, also a pilot, was adamant that flying for me was an impossibility. He went on and on about it. But that only fuelled the desire and I guess, in a strange way, he did me a favour. Nevertheless, I enjoyed the day I landed in front of him, spun around and gave him a little wave as I taxied past. I've never seen him since.

It's now a decade since I've flown my ultralight. Eventually the novelty wore off and I'd only fly if someone wanted me to take them up. As my life grew busier on the farm, I found I had less and less time for flying, until one day I finally stopped. My ultralight days may be over, but it's only a matter of time before I'll take to the sky again – that's something for the future.

Meanwhile, I'll carry that view from the top of my own Mount Kosciusko with me forever.

NINE

JUST ME AND MY DOGS

By the 1990s I had reclaimed my life. I was living reasonably independently, helping on the farm, could fly an ultralight and was enjoying my social life. But still there was something missing.

The view from the top of my mountain was pretty spectacular but, like anything, it's always better if you can share it with someone else. I didn't have a female companion to share this rebuilt life with, someone to grow old with, to share the highs and lows, to work with side by side, day in, day out. I wanted someone to wake up to every morning, to be able to roll over and wrap my arms around. Someone to watch the sunset with, sitting on the verandah with a beer at the end of the day. To share a joke with. Someone to chase my goals with, to restore an old house with. Someone to love. I felt I had an enormous amount of love to give.

As the years passed, I began to think it wasn't going to happen. I watched all my mates get married and have kids and I observed from the sidelines – happy for them, increasingly sad for me.

148

Often I sat among the guests at the reception and looked at the bride and groom and wondered if it would ever be me sitting up there, grinning from ear to ear.

But like most things in my life, I accepted it. There was no point in yearning for something I couldn't have, so I focussed on what I had. I imagined life with just me and my dogs. I'd continue to live with Mum and Dad and they'd care for me and when they weren't around any more, then Bill and Kate might look after me, or I'd find someone else.

Don't get me wrong, I wasn't a complete monk throughout those years. I had relationships with two or three girls but mostly they fell in love with Sam. When they got to know his mate quadriplegia, it wasn't for them.

The issue wasn't simply them accepting my injury. It was also about me getting past the fear that I would place too much of a burden on their life. I had to come to terms with what I couldn't contribute to a relationship, and I would have to live with that frustration and knowledge every day. It was like having a little voice in the back of my head reminding me every now and again of my shortcomings. As a man with spinal injury, it was hard to cope with not being able to do the heavy work. The little things like loading luggage into a car, mowing the lawn, changing a flat tyre – all the jobs the male tended to do. For me, that included things around the farm as well.

And of course, there was sex – or the lack of it. The majority of men who suffer a spinal cord injury also lose the ability to control their erections. The effect of every spinal cord injury is different, but generally it completely changes your sex life. From very early on I worried about it. Eventually I discovered that, because I felt virtually no sensation or stimulation from my injury down, I too didn't get an erection normally. I could still get one but not necessarily at the right time and it was not to be relied upon. Like an old lawnmower that had seen better days, I didn't know when it would start and when it wouldn't. You could bet your boots that when the grass was most in need of a cut, it would fail me. This didn't do much for my self-esteem and left me wondering if I could ever satisfy a woman sexually. I felt I'd lost my manhood, my masculinity, and I was inadequate. And down the track, there were questions about whether I'd be able to father children – another big sacrifice for most women.

So my injury wasn't only about the loss of mobility. It was also about the loss of sexual function, bowel and bladder, temperature control, being able to father my own kids, kick them a football or help with the day-to-day jobs that a male normally does in the household. It was about being the man about the house and being a role model. It was going to take a pretty extraordinary girl to take all that on. She'd have to be willing to accept all the things I couldn't do. In a sense, she'd be partly taking on a spinal injury herself, but on top of that, she would have to deal with extra tasks, things a husband might otherwise do.

As if that wasn't a tall enough order, I faced an extra dilemma. I wanted to settle down with a country girl – someone who would want to help me on the farm, but I knew that would almost certainly mean she'd be keen on other outdoor activities too, most of which I wouldn't be able to share. She'd probably want to ride horses, which I couldn't do. If she liked sport or bushwalking or canoeing, it would be difficult for me to do it with her.

It seemed an impossible dream – finding all the things I needed in one girl. Then I had to be lucky enough to meet her, and teach her all about spinal cord injury and its complications without scaring her off. It was the stuff that fantasies were made of.

While I accepted my fate, I didn't completely give up all hope that my dream might come true, and it was fuelled by a conversation I had one day.

I was staying with an old school friend whose grandmother was visiting. We were talking about finding that special person to spend our lives with, and I said I wondered if I ever would. The old lady was surrounded by her brood of grandchildren – the physical evidence of a long and family-filled life. She'd seen romance and love, marriage and childbirth. Hers was a life full of memories, both happy and sad, and the wisdom that these brought.

'Sam, you'll meet a very special girl one day,' she said. There was no doubt in her mind. I carried those words with me from that moment on. They gave me hope that maybe, just maybe, she might be right.

Another person gave me hope. He was Mike Warden, a C5/6 quadriplegic who lived in Tamworth, about three hours' drive away. He became one of my best friends and a great mentor. We first met in 1991 and from that time on he was such an inspiration to me. Our lives had many parallels. We had both suffered spinal injuries in car accidents early in our lives, me at nineteen years of age, Mike at twenty-one. We both loved the bush and chose to go back home to the land after our injuries and live life as normally as possible with a positive attitude. Those similarities were like a magnet between us.

But Mike was perhaps most amazing because he had suffered his injury way back in 1952, before the days of specialist spinal units and the drugs and medical technology and expertise we take for granted today. After his accident he was taken to Tamworth Hospital, where he was placed in a plaster jacket from head to waist. Like me, he was left with no temperature control and it was the middle of January. He sweltered in forty-degree Celsius temperatures with no airconditioning. A couple of weeks later he was flown to Sydney for an operation on his neck. His plane was late and Mike lay waiting on a stretcher in a tin shed, still encased in plaster. He waited like that in horrendous heat for more than an hour. The fact he survived at all was an amazing feat and credit to his own personal determination and stamina.

Mike says he was lucky because it was just after the Korean War and medical staff were starting to learn more about spinal injuries and how to treat them. But when I consider how I was rushed within two days to a fully operational, state-of-the-art spinal unit with specialist doctors, nurses, physiotherapists and occupational therapists, I think how lucky I was. Of course, today there's even more knowledge about the injury and I'm sure it will be only a matter of time before researchers make it possible to operate on spinal cord injuries and patients will walk out of hospitals within weeks.

In Mike's case, the enthusiastic Tamworth hospital staff did everything they could to make his life as productive as possible. Within six months he returned to the family farm, and after his parents died he helped run it, getting around on a small tractor, similar in size to a ride-on mower.

Snow skiing at Thredbo with my instructor Eddie.

Jenny's kelpie Winkie jumped up on my car door and licked my arm the first time we met, which Jenny said was very unusual – her dog never normally took to anyone that quickly. I thought, 'I wish you'd take some bloody lessons from your dog!'

Jenny on our wedding day with Mike and Marg Warden, whose love story inspired me to hope I might find someone one day.

Our wedding day in March 1999. Reverend Bill Howarth and the TAS chapel are in the background.

Me with my sister Kate and brother Bill at his wedding in 2002.

Jenny and me mustering together in 1999. (Photo: Libor Sikora)

'You're not going to leave me up here, are you?' – Jenny helping me into the header. (Photo: Mike Lowe)

Not many get away. (Photo: Mike Lowe)

The slasher attached to the front of my bike. (Photo: Mike Lowe)

With Jenny and Minty – the two girls in my life take a ride on my bike.
(Photo: Mike Lowe)

'Australian Story' crew: cameraman Anthony Sines, producer Caitlin Shea and editor Roger Carter during a break from filming 'Small World' in 2004.

Me with Deb Fleming, executive producer of 'Australian Story' in Brisbane in late 2005.

Then in the early 1990s, after being single for most of his life, he married Marg, a nurse who he first met in 1966 at Tamworth Base Hospital. At the time she was married with three boys, but Mike became a special family friend. She sat by his bedside in 1990 when he was so ill he almost died and their friendship blossomed into something more. I visited Mike and Marg constantly throughout the 1990s and did the honours as best man at their wedding.

Their love story gave me so much hope, letting me know that it was possible for someone to love another person, despite a severe disability and all its associated challenges. Marg told me one day, 'Wait until you're thirty, Sam. You won't find anyone until you're thirty.'

And so, despite all the odds, deep down in my heart I never gave up hope. I trusted that if I met the right girl, she wouldn't mind my mate quadriplegia. That she'd be able to see past the wheelchair and my inability to do a few things, and see just me.

Meanwhile, I wasn't sitting at home moping. In the winter of 1991 I went skiing at Thredbo. A family friend, Paul Griffiths, was heavily involved with disabled skiing in Australia and invited me to go to the snow with his family. He also organised lessons for me with the school for disabled skiers. It was fantastic and I will be forever in his debt. I had a terrific instructor called Eddie, who rode shotgun behind me for the first four days while I learnt to balance myself on a sitski, which was like a wheelchair without wheels. Instead it slid on a single ski about two-and-a-half metres long and eight centimetres wide. I helped balance and manoeuvre myself with little outriggers on both arms – like crutches with tiny skis on the ends – but it was pretty difficult with no trunk muscles. We added a harness and ropes to tie me in, and that helped, but it wasn't easy.

I started on Friday Flat, the beginners' slope and I spent most of the week there. Eddie taught me how to stay upright and helped me get back up when I fell, which I did regularly. The chairlift was pretty scary to start with as well, but I eventually mastered that. Probably the worst thing was the cold. By the end of each day I was freezing and it would take me half the night to warm up again. But I still had a great time. I'll never forget going down the slope on the fourth day, thinking Eddie was behind me helping and suddenly halfway down the hill he skied past me. I'd thought he was holding me up.

What a feeling, flowing down the icy slope with the wind in my face and those mountains around me. I'd finally mastered it, or so I thought. The next day we decided to try a more difficult slope, which proved to be way beyond me, so it was back to the beginner's flat ... and a few more days perfecting my skills. Nevertheless by the end of the week I was really getting the hang of it, and knew that, with a bit more practice I would have been ready for a more challenging slope, but it was time to go home. There are better disabled skis available now – they come with two skis rather than one, so it would be a lot more stable. I'm sure I'll give it another try one day.

My next big adventure was travelling overseas. My uncle, Philip Bailey, and my cousin, Georgie Bailey, were both living in England at the time, so I instantly had a base to travel from and contacts through them. Philip did some research for me and sent information over to help me plan the trip, and I talked a friend into going with me. She provided some backup because she worked in the medical profession and was familiar with the treatment of spinal injury.

But it was daunting, leaving behind the security of my home country for the first time, with all its medical facilities, our common language and its familiarity. It really hit home when I was sitting in the jumbo about to take off for our first stopover in the Philippines. For a few moments I did wonder, 'What are you doing this for?' because I really was severing my lifelines. If something serious happened while I was in another country, I wasn't sure if I could get the same level of medical expertise I was accustomed to in Australia. I went through my list of essentials like drugs and catheters dozens of times to make sure I had everything, and hoped like hell that my wheelchair didn't go missing in transit.

The two nights in the Philippines confirmed some of my concerns. Even though we'd asked for a room with disabled access and booked a first-class motel thinking that would help, the room wasn't at all suitable. We had to remove one wheel from my wheelchair to get it through the bathroom door. The next morning I thought, 'Shit, what have I done?'

But things improved once we got to London and we travelled throughout England, Scotland, Wales and Ireland without any major problems. In fact, that trip was one of the greatest experiences of my life. Many of the old castles and buildings had ramps and some provided scooters, which were fantastic. With a scooter, I could get around and see everything easily, including the Dover wartime tunnels – an absolute highlight. After we discovered a motel chain that provided reliable accessible rooms, we often stayed with them as we travelled. It was a bit like McDonalds fast food restaurants – love the food or hate it, you always knew what you were getting.

As luck would have it, we also managed to get our hands on a set of portable hand controls for a motor car. We were able to use them on the vehicle we hired and they were easy to put on and off. A rod was attached to the brake at one end and there was a handle at the other, a bit like the curved handle of a walking stick. It rested near my right knee. Under my thumb there was a button, which activated a second rod attached to the accelerator. The whole thing was held in place by a Velcro strap around the steering column. It was brilliant. So simple yet so effective.

Phil and his good friend Tim Coupland owned a Mercedes, which was their pride and joy. I decided to try the hand controls on it, so Phil reluctantly put them on and I climbed in. He was looking extremely nervous. Here was Sam about to try these new hand controls for the first time ever in his prized possession and as we backed out the driveway, I could see how tense he was.

'We won't go out on the highway,' he said. 'We'll just go down this back road.'

So I started off and I intentionally jerked the car and spun the wheels, all the while watching the horrified expression on Phil's face. 'Don't worry, I'm in total control,' I said. His face turned ashen. Then he saw me laughing. I don't think that helped much. He was mighty relieved when we got back to the house safely, and immediately removed the hand controls from his beloved Merc. I didn't put a scratch on his car but he never offered it to me again. But Phil and Tim welcomed us with open arms and I could never have done the trip as easily without their convenient and welcoming home base.

As I said once before, there are moments in your life when a split-second decision can change the path you follow forever. I had another experience like that in the winter of 1995.

One afternoon the phone rang. It was a guy called Shane Mahony, the presenter of ABC Radio's daily rural program, the *Country Hour*. He was ringing from Sydney and had heard about me while speaking to someone at the Rural Health Unit in Moree. It was coming up to Farm Safety Week and Shane was looking for someone to interview. He asked me if I'd do something with him over the phone for the *Country Hour*.

'I'd rather not do it over the phone, if you don't mind,' I said. 'Is there any chance someone could come up here and meet me?'

Don't ask me why I said that. I look back now and it's eerie. I'd done lots of radio interviews over the phone in the past. In fact, I'd never asked to do it face-to-face before that day. I'd just try to paint a picture as best as I could over the phone – and that was it. I never thought twice about it.

But there I was that winter afternoon saying no. It seems even more bizarre now looking back because it was the first time it was for a truly rural program – the others had been with city radio stations. I must have had rocks in my head. But perhaps it was fate. Like the day I decided to go to the pub in Camooweal all those Sundays ago, the day I had my accident and completely changed the direction of my life forever. Some things just seem to be meant to happen.

'It's terribly difficult to describe over the phone how my hoist works, or how I get on or off my bike and the other things I do around the farm. I think it would be much more beneficial if someone could actually come and see it for themselves.'

'That's no trouble at all,' said Shane. 'I can totally understand that. Leave it with me and someone will get back in touch.'

We said goodbye and as I put down the phone I thought, 'That'll be the last I'll hear of him.'

But I was wrong. A few days later the phone rang and a young woman introduced herself. 'Hi, I'm Jenny Black from ABC Radio. Shane Mahony suggested I give you a call. I was wondering if I could come up and do an interview?' You could have bowled me over with a feather.

We started to chat. Pretty soon I discovered we'd both grown up on the land and there was an instant connection. We immediately shared a common language and interests. There was also this bubbly, smiley voice that came through the phone and grabbed me. Sparks flew down the phone line straightaway.

I arranged for Jenny to come to Bardin the following week and gave her directions. I hung up the phone, seriously impressed, and went looking for Mum.

'Have you ever heard of Jenny Black?'

'She's with ABC Radio, isn't she? We've been listening to Jenny for quite a few years. She does a program on the ABC in Tamworth every morning before the seven o'clock news. It's quite interesting. She often talks to people we know … from the New England Northwest area.'

So the next morning, yours truly gave the local FM music station the flick and tuned into ABC Radio in Tamworth.

It was Jenny's voice that first captivated me. It bubbled out of the radio and made me want to listen. Like a good working dog, it headed me off and rounded me up and wouldn't let me escape. She sounded cheerful and fun and had this infectious giggle. I started painting a picture of what she looked like. For some reason I imagined she was quite tall and had dark hair and an olive complexion. As I listened through the week she got taller and taller and better and better-looking.

When the day of Jenny's visit finally arrived I was very excited. I decided to meet her at the front ramp, and I sat there in the cool, mid-afternoon sun – not a cloud in the sky – with my three dogs, Dusty, Missy, and Jaffa, on the back of the bike. I'd been waiting about ten minutes when I saw a swirl of dust slowly rising in the distance. A white station wagon turned off Croppa Creek Road and drove up the driveway, over our front ramp.

As the vehicle came closer I eagerly peered through the windscreen. Straightaway the long-anticipated dark, olive complexion disappeared; there was a reddish reflection through the glass.

Jenny pulled up and wound down the car window. 'Hello, you must be Sam.'

She looked completely the opposite of what I was expecting. I don't mean I was disappointed – shocked is probably more like it – because she was nothing like I'd imagined.

These are Jenny's recollections of that first time we saw each other: 'I remember thinking he was very handsome, with his suntanned face – its colour deepened by the cold wind. He wore a large, thick faded green coat. It made him look big, cuddly and strong. Was it love at first sight? I don't think so – I took my job very seriously and I was there to do an interview.'

We introduced ourselves and chatted. One thing I noticed almost immediately was how close the driver's seat was to the steering wheel – it was less than thirty centimetres away – so I quickly put two and two together and figured out Jenny wasn't going to be especially tall either.

I followed her car up to the house. She parked it under the shade of a gnarled old pepper tree while I put my bike in the shed and jumped across into my chair. As Jenny got out of the car, I spun around and was amazed to see a red-haired, freckly-faced, sawn-off little runt. But she was the best-looking red-haired, freckly-faced, sawn-off little runt I'd ever laid eyes on. There was a spark right from the very start.

But I still couldn't get over how short she was. I was used to being surrounded by tall people. My parents are tall and I was 188 centimetres before my accident. Jenny was only 157 centimetres.

Throughout the afternoon Jenny recorded my story on tape. She asked me about my life so far, the accident, what I did on the farm and how I did it. We talked about my injury and about quadriplegia, and the challenges I faced living on the land. She recorded the sounds of me getting on and off different pieces of equipment and driving away on the motorbike. The interview was completely unlike those I'd done before. In the past I'd spoken on city radio stations to people who didn't know anything about farming or life on the land. Often they didn't know the difference between a bull and a steer or a wheat crop and barley crop, so a lot of their questions didn't really hit the right spot. Jenny was a whole different ball game. She understood farming life and asked relevant questions.

After we'd finished recording I did something that maybe was indicative of how I felt about this girl I'd only just met. On that cold, blustery winter day, I attempted to take Jenny over to Pine Hills, the adjoining property we'd bought a few years earlier and where, if I ever married, I imagined I would live. She was doing a series of radio items on interesting shearing sheds in the region and I thought she might like to see the shed there. We set off on my four-wheel bike as the sun was setting and the wind turning icy. We'd gone about a fifth of the six-kilometre journey when I decided to turn back, despite Jenny's assurances she wasn't too cold. I suspect she was secretly relieved – and she had no idea we still had so far to go. She would have been an icicle by the time we got back home.

It was dark when we returned and Jenny had an hour's drive ahead of her back to her motel in Moree. But with a bit of help and persuasion from my parents, I talked her into staying with us instead. That night we sat around the fire, Mum, Dad, Jenny and me. We talked about agriculture, the season, grain and cattle prices, politics, all sorts of things. I hardly got a word in edgeways. In fact, the only time I spent alone with Jenny that night was when we went into the quiet of my bedroom to record some more for the interview. Finally, we could talk, just the two of us. Later that night I lay in bed and thought, 'What a great girl.'

She left early the next morning but she stayed prominently in my thoughts for days. I couldn't wait to see how the interview would turn out, but Jenny had also had a big impact on me personally. It wasn't love at first sight, but she'd certainly gained a new member of her fan club.

I thought about Jenny a lot over the next couple of years. It was hard not to because I'd turn on the radio in the morning and there she was. Often she'd be interviewing someone I knew. I didn't think about her all the time, but every now and again we'd speak on the phone or she'd come to the area doing interviews and she'd stay the night. It would rekindle the friendship.

And so we got to know each other better and better. I found out Jenny was a keen horse rider, competing in one-day eventing and dressage, and loved to go bushwalking and camping. I wondered whether a deeper relationship was possible but dismissed the idea because I thought she'd have to give up her horses and other outdoor interests if she ended up with me. I couldn't ask her to do that. Anyway, I imagined a terrific girl like Jenny would have a boyfriend and, if she didn't, she'd have plenty chasing her. Why would she rather have me?

It wasn't only that. Hot summers and cold winters would never be the same for her if she shared my life – thanks to my inability to tolerate the heat and cold. And I wondered whether she'd be willing to do most of the physical work around the place – the mowing, packing and unpacking the car or fixing broken water pipes or pumps. It seemed safer for me to do nothing.

Meanwhile, the interview was broadcast on Jenny's ABC regional radio program in the New England Northwest, then repeated on *Country Hour* programs across the nation and it even went internationally on Radio Australia. It drew an enormous response.

Despite all my misgivings about relationships, I did seek Jenny out on a couple of occasions. One night I really wanted to phone her. She had a silent number at home, which she'd given me and I kept it in my electronic personal organiser. But when I turned it on, its batteries were going flat. I could just make out Jenny's name, but I couldn't read the last three digits of her phone number. At that stage, I didn't know any of Jenny's friends and it was after hours so I couldn't ring the ABC to get her number.

Then I had a brainwave. I remembered how the heat on the dashboard of my car had helped boost the batteries the weekend before. I thought, 'I just need to heat it up a bit.' So I put it in the microwave and gave it a quick zap. I only gave it a few seconds. A puff of blue smoke instantly filled the interior. F … ! I opened the door of the microwave and a foul smell and smoke flooded the kitchen. I'd bloody cooked it. It's not a story I tell proudly, but it proved Jenny had some sort of spell over me because I certainly wasn't thinking straight.

The next morning, sheepishly, I rang the ABC.

'ABC Radio, can I help you?' It was Jenny's workmate and the breakfast presenter, Bill Gleeson.

'It's Sam Bailey speaking.'

'Hello, Sam. How's things at Croppa Creek?'

We chatted for a while, then I said, 'What I'm really ringing for is Jenny Black's phone number and I know it's probably not protocol for you to give it out …'

But Bill very quickly interrupted, 'Oh no, I'm sure she wouldn't mind if I gave you her phone number.'

So he did and I rang her. I didn't tell her the story about the electronic organiser until a long time after. I was far too embarrassed.

Whenever I spoke to Jenny we talked for ages. When I got off the phone I was always floating on cloud nine. The first thing I felt like doing was ringing her straight back.

Eventually I plucked up the courage to ask her out. I was staying with Mike and Marg in Tamworth and it was the week of the Country Music Festival. We were having breakfast one morning when Mike mentioned he'd bought a copy of a book Jenny had written for ABC Books called *The Country's Finest Hour – Fifty Years of Rural Broadcasting*. He thought it'd be nice to have Jenny sign it. I thought to myself, 'You beauty!'

It was a brilliant opportunity. I was always trying to think of reasons to contact her, but I didn't want to show my cards too much. I still didn't want to look too keen in case she didn't feel the same way. Mike had just given me the perfect excuse. I rang and arranged to take the book around to be signed. I couldn't grab the book and get out that door fast enough.

As I left, Mike gave me careful instructions. 'Could you get Jenny to sign it Mike? I hate "Michael" and I really loathe "Mick."'

It was lucky I didn't pass a police car – I sped the whole way. It was the first time I'd been to Jenny's home on the outskirts of town and I hadn't seen her for quite a while. She walked out the front door to meet me and again I was amazed at how short she was. We chatted and eventually I thought, here goes. I took a deep breath.

'Jenny, what are you doing for lunch? There's probably a band on somewhere down the street we could go and see. Would you like to have lunch?'

'You wouldn't believe it, but I've got some friends staying for the Country Music Festival and we're all going to a barbecue. Sorry, Sam, I can't.'

Damn! Well, that didn't work … now to plan B. I took another deep breath. 'What about tonight, Jenny? Are you doing anything tonight? The Bushwackers are playing at the Long Yard Hotel, maybe we could go there.'

'Oh, sorry Sam, I've got to cover the national rodeo finals tonight for my program in the morning.'

Unbelievable!

I was so deflated; talk about letting the air out of the tyre. But I wasn't completely defeated because I was thinking, surely if she had any feelings for me at all, the immediate response would be to ask me what I was doing the next day or next weekend or something. Nothing. She didn't say a thing. Quite obviously she wasn't interested in pursuing anything more than a friendship with me. And I still didn't know if she had another bloke.

We chatted for a bit longer, with me sitting there in my ute feeling like a failed sponge cake. All the while Jenny's black and tan kelpie dog, Winkie, had been lying under the shade of a nearby tree. Suddenly, she wandered over to the car and jumped up, putting both front paws on the window sill. She gently licked my arm.

Jenny was stunned. 'That's amazing. My dog never normally takes to anyone that quickly.'

'Well, I wish you'd take some bloody lessons from your dog,' I thought.

After that, there wasn't much reason to stay. I gave her the book, asked her to sign it and I left.

As I climbed out of the ute at Mike's place and reached for the book, I tried to console myself that at least the trip achieved one thing. I glanced inside the cover to see what Jenny had written and you wouldn't believe it, she'd written 'Dear Mick'. So I had to go in and apologise to Mike and explain what had happened. What a dud trip. To tell the truth, I didn't really enjoy any of the Country Music Festival that year.

The experience certainly didn't erase the image I had of myself growing old. The picture of me in my wheelchair sitting alone on the verandah, with only my dogs for company, was still well and truly in place.

TEN

SHE'S A CRACKER!

One of the really great things about life is you never know what's around the corner. You can be convinced that all hope of happiness or fulfilment of a goal or resolution of a problem is lost, and then out of the blue everything changes.

For me that happened when the phone rang one night and it was Jenny. She had some interviews to do in Moree early the next Monday morning and planned to spend the previous night there. She wanted to know if I'd like to go in for dinner.

This time the boot was on the other foot. 'Look, we're pretty busy out here,' I said. 'We've just finished harvest and we're delivering wheat ... but leave it with me.' We arranged for Jenny to ring me on Sunday. I hung up, knowing I'd be in Moree before her.

To be honest I was over the moon because until then she'd always visited me at home when Mum and Dad were there. As I've mentioned earlier, I used to struggle to get a word in edgeways. Finally I'd have Jenny all to myself.

Actually what I had planned was to spend the weekend in Brisbane, partly to pick up a new cattle dog pup. I went ahead with that, caught up with a few mates and had a big night out on Saturday. Although I was pretty hung over, I wanted to be home for Jenny's phone call. So with both eyes propped open with the proverbial matchsticks, I slowly drove home with the little pup beside me on the passenger's side floor, peeing and pooing at regular intervals. The smell didn't blend very well with my already seedy stomach, I can tell you. How I didn't throw up I'll never know but at least it kept me awake. And all the way home I was thinking, 'She'll want to ring or I'll kill her.'

One of the first things Mum said when I wheeled in the door was, 'Oh, by the way, Jenny Black rang.' In a flash I recovered. The nausea was gone and I was full of energy, wide awake.

Jenny and I had a great dinner. We drank lots of red wine, laughed and talked and I felt I'd known her forever. For the first time we talked about relationships. I told her how I hadn't yet found the right person to share my life with and, funnily enough, she said the same thing. She told me what she was looking for in a man, and I thought, 'That's me! You're looking at him!' I wanted to shout it from the rooftops. But I didn't know whether she was talking about me or just talking to me as a friend.

When we left the restaurant, I reached for Jenny's hand. 'Come on, you can pull me along.' It was the first time we'd touched. She held my hand and pulled me along the footpath. Surely she'll stop and ask me into her room for a cup of coffee or something. But she didn't. She dragged me straight past the room to my ute. I couldn't believe it. As far as she was concerned, it was obviously time to go.

While I thought the night had ended on a low note, for Jenny it was quite the opposite. Looking back on it, she said, 'It never occurred to me to ask Sam into my room. After all, I had a big day ahead of me the next day. But I do remember Sam's hand brushing the inside of my wrist as we chatted at the car. It was like an electric shock.'

It was after midnight when we parted. Although I didn't want to leave, all good things come to an end. I don't remember much of the trip home. I was floating. I didn't see the road as it disappeared under the wheels. For the first time I thought this friendship might have the potential to be something much more.

That night I went to sleep dreaming about Jenny. In the euphoria of spending the evening with her I'd forgotten about my wheelchair. But bugger it, next morning I woke and there was my mate quadriplegia.

While this battle went on inside my head, Christmas drew near and that year I had a special reason to smile. During our dinner in Moree I'd given Jenny a small box of chocolates wrapped in Christmas paper with a card, and felt I'd touched a spot with her. Little could I know they'd sit on the dashboard of her car for ten hours the next day, and then again on the trip home to her parents for Christmas before they would be finally opened. They'd melted many times over by then, but it was the thought that counted.

And Jenny sent me a Christmas gift as well. Because my present wasn't very big, she'd decided on something fun, rather than expensive. She rang on Christmas Day to discover that our family all sit around and watch each other open their presents. She was mortified to think they sat and watched me open hers –

a plastic bathtub plug attached by chain to a green rubber frog! Of course everyone had been fascinated to find out what was in this parcel from Jenny Black and it took up more than the normal amount of interest. Someone summed it up with, 'Oh well, that's different.' Jenny was horrified but I thought it was the best present I received that year.

During the following week Jenny and I spoke a number of times on the phone and after each call it became harder and harder to hang up. It was amazing. We never ran out of things to say to each other. Sometimes we'd be there for an hour or two at a time. Perhaps the most memorable phone call was on New Year's Eve. Neither of us were doing anything so we agreed to talk at midnight. We got on the phone and chatted and laughed and talked about our dreams and aspirations. When we eventually said goodbye it was 2am – we'd been on the phone for two hours but it had felt like five minutes.

I hung up and thought yet again, 'What a great girl!' We were gradually getting to know each other's likes and dislikes, hobbies and interests. But whenever we talked about Jenny's passion for horses, I felt that little seed of doubt.

A few days later, on the spur of the moment, I decided to send Jenny some flowers but I didn't want to look too keen. I was keeping Jenny up to date with my new pup, which I'd named Wheelie, for obvious reasons. She was a dog lover and thought he sounded pretty cute. So rather than go out on a limb myself, I decided to send the first bunch of flowers on behalf of Wheelie. I rang the florist, organised a bunch and put on the card, 'Wheelie thinks you're great.' I sent them to the ABC studios and waited to see the reaction.

That night the phone rang and I knew I'd hit the mark. Jenny was delighted. So the next few days I bombarded the ABC with flowers, much to the curiosity of all the other staff.

Jenny said later, 'I was busy at my desk when this big bouquet of flowers arrived at the front counter and I hardly gave it a thought. Generally when flowers arrived, they were for the breakfast announcer Bill Gleeson, who did a lot in the community and was very popular. So I was amazed when the girl from the florist said they were for me. As soon as I read the card, I knew they were from Sam and I was so chuffed. I'd never really been given flowers much before, so it was a pretty special gesture and of course, it made me start thinking about a more serious relationship with Sam – maybe we could be more than just friends after all.'

While the reaction to the flowers had given me more confidence, I still wasn't certain if Jenny was seeing someone else or how she felt about me. She hadn't said anything, so I wasn't sure. But I'd been given enough encouragement not to give up.

At the end of January I headed down to Tamworth for the Country Music Festival yet again, for my usual three or four days with Mike and Marg. Some great friends near Gunnedah, about an hour from Tamworth, asked me for lunch and I invited Jenny. She knew the family because she'd often interviewed both the father and son for her radio program.

They were very close friends of mine, in fact one of the three daughters was a former girlfriend and I'd occasionally spent weekends with the family. We sat at a huge long table for lunch, the three girls near me at one end and Jenny at the other end with their mother; other family members were in between.

At our end of the table we were having a ball, talking and laughing and the girls were wrapping their arms around me. Little did I know Jenny was down the other end green with envy. I wasn't trying to make her jealous. I was just having fun with great mates but Jenny didn't know what to think. Like me, she still didn't know exactly how I felt about her and was left wondering if I just wanted to be friends, despite the Christmas gift and flowers. That lunch proved to be the catalyst that made her realise how much she cared. It wasn't planned that way but in the end those friends did me an enormous favour. Jenny had finally acknowledged to herself that she was falling for me.

She shouldn't really have been surprised. Some of her friends had picked it a mile away. Jenny was in her early thirties and, like me, wondering whether she was going to find the man of her dreams. Once when she was discussing this with a close friend, her friend said, 'What about Sam Bailey? You always speak about him differently to everyone else.' A workmate asked her a similar question on another occasion. But still she couldn't see it, even though I was right under her nose.

After the lunch near Gunnedah we headed back to Mike and Marg's for dinner, where Jenny was a huge hit. In fact, there was an immediate connection because Mike's cousin happened to be the doctor Jenny's family had had while she was growing up at Scone. Mike and Marg say they knew straightaway that Jenny was the right girl for me and when I climbed into the ute to take her home, Mike gave me a wink.

When I got to Jenny's place I parked in the driveway and we chatted … and chatted … and chatted. We were getting closer and closer, but this time I was the one who didn't make a move. 'I've got to go,' I announced all of a sudden. 'I'll talk to you a bit later.'

When I got back to Mike and Marg's, they couldn't believe it. 'What're you doing home so early? We didn't expect you home for ages.'

I didn't kiss Jenny that night. It wasn't because I was unsure of my feelings but I still didn't know how she felt. I'd held her hand after dinner in Moree, given her a Christmas gift, sent her flowers and taken her to lunch and dinner, but I hadn't received any clear signs from her about how she felt.

Jenny says, 'Isn't it funny? The messages you think you're giving out can be very different from reality. I remember leaning towards Sam while we were chatting in the car, thinking I was giving him plenty of opportunity to kiss me. I would have thought my interest was pretty plain, but obviously it wasn't. Too many years of playing the dating game makes you wary. Perhaps I'd been putting people off for years. Not that it mattered because it wasn't until I met Sam that I knew I'd met the right person.'

Even if Jenny's signals had been clearer, I might not have been ready. There was still part of me that had to come to terms with my own injury and whether I could put the burden of my physical limitations onto someone else for the rest of their life. During the next four days I battled within myself over whether I could or couldn't pursue the relationship.

While I'd casually mentioned to Jenny about coming up the following weekend, that week passed and I didn't get in touch. She was getting the strong message that this friendship wasn't going anywhere. As each night passed with no phone call, she was becoming more convinced I didn't feel the same way and her overwhelming sense of disappointment surprised her. Again it reinforced just how much she was falling for me.

For my part, I was completely rapt in her – but again I'd forgotten about the wheelchair. I oscillated between thinking I could go ahead with the relationship and then thinking I couldn't – that I couldn't load up Jenny with my disability. It was all a bit traumatic. I'd lie in bed at night tossing from one thought to another. Could I? Should I not? And anyway, did she even like me? Around and around I went.

Then one morning I awoke and thought, 'Sam Bailey, what are you mucking around for? This isn't the Sam Bailey I know – you've never backed away from anything in your life.' That night I rang Jenny and the joy came right down the phone. I could tell she was terribly excited and it was such a relief. Not only because Jenny was so pleased to hear from me, but because I'd made a decision to give it a go.

When Jenny arrived at Bardin she handed me a card. It read, 'Winkie thinks you're gorgeous. She thinks about you all the time, and she loves your smile … and so do I.' She signed it 'Lots of love, Jenny.'

That weekend we finally kissed for the first time. We talked about my concerns about my disability. I told her more about my injury and how it affected my bowel and bladder and temperature control and of course with time we found out about the sexual effects of quadriplegia.

What made our deepening relationship so incredible for me was that Jenny was so easy to talk to. Unusually for someone with no exposure to spinal injury, she seemed undaunted by it all. Most often if spinal-injured people marry, it's to a nurse or physio or occupational therapist or someone in the medical profession, because they are less likely to find it confronting. So it was unexpected that Jenny took it all in her stride.

She explains for herself: 'Before I met Sam, the only people I'd ever known in a wheelchair were old and sick. But by the time Sam and I spent that first weekend together, the wheelchair had disappeared. And during those couple of years we were friends, I'd gone out with guys who could walk and run and even ride horses, but there was always something missing. The feelings weren't right. There was no way I was going to walk away from the love of my life just because he couldn't walk and do a few other things.

'Every one of us has things we can't do for lots of different reasons. They might be due to family or work pressures, or because of financial, physical or psychological limitations. You might want to play cricket for Australia, but you can't bat or bowl well enough. You might want to build a house, but you don't have the skills or the strength.

'It's about accepting your limitations and aspiring to achieve the things we can do. For example, it would be difficult for Sam and me to go bushwalking and camping together, a pastime I used to enjoy, but it doesn't matter because I got to do that earlier in my life. Now we choose, most of the time, to do the things we can do together, and there are lots of them. I don't focus on the things we can't do because there's so many things we can do, and we aren't going to be able to fit all of them into a lifetime.'

Jenny says she realised by the end of that first weekend together she'd found something very special and within a couple of weeks she knew she would spend the rest of her life with me.

She once asked a school friend's mum, 'How do you know when you've met the right person to marry?'

'You just know.'

'How do you know?'

'You just do.'

After going out with me for only a few weeks, Jenny finally understood what her friend's mum meant. She said, 'It taught me, if you don't know, it's not the right person.'

When Jenny left after that first weekend I'd gone through my own psychological sea change. Yet again, my world had shifted on its axis and I'd reaffirmed that nothing was impossible.

I found out in the end it didn't matter that I was disabled. It didn't matter that my bladder didn't work or that I was restricted by the weather or couldn't do all those other things. When you find the right person it's irrelevant, whereas it had been a massive concern before. And in the end I realised it was my burden alone to carry and I figured that if it was okay with Jenny, it was okay with me.

I couldn't believe my luck. I'd fulfilled that final dream. She had red hair and freckles and wasn't very tall but she was an absolute bloody cracker!

ELEVEN

A 'LIVE' PROPOSAL

One of my rules of life is to do things differently. If someone jumps a fence a certain way, then I'll go out of my way to do it another – sometimes no doubt to my detriment. But I was brought up to be creative and unique. It's important to push the boundaries of thinking, challenge the way things are done and question everything.

It's not about being an exhibitionist or trying to stand out from a crowd for the sake of my ego – it's about not becoming one of the masses. It's about not conforming or being told what and how to think. It's a fairly typical Australian trait – and my childhood in the bush encouraged that independence, the desire to do things my way.

Well, when it came to making Jenny's and my relationship official, I thought I'd like to do something different. It occurred to me that with Jenny being on the radio, I had a glorious opportunity. So I put my thinking cap on and came up with an idea.

But first I needed to speak to Jenny's parents, Norman and Noelene. I knew that at our age I wasn't expected to ask them for her hand in marriage – a lot of people didn't any more. But I wanted to because I thought it was the right thing to do, and it was what all my mates had done. In fact, they'd described it as one of the most traumatic things they'd ever had to do. Even though I'd heard this over and over from different friends, I'd been sure they were as weak as water. 'Oh, you bloody pussycats. What's wrong with you?'

Now it was my turn to find out how I would cope. An occasion presented itself within weeks. Jenny's parents were going to be showing their Cairns terriers at a dog show at Manilla, half an hour north of Tamworth. The same weekend Jenny was attending an art workshop at Barraba, passing through Manilla on the way. It was the perfect opening.

Everything went according to plan. Jenny dropped me off in Manilla, no doubt wondering why in the world I'd want to spend the whole day at the dog show. An hour or two was one thing, but a whole day?

All I had to do was enjoy a yarn, watch a few parading dogs, pop the question and the task was complete. But it turned out to be easier said then done. All day I sat there, biding my time, waiting for the right moment. There were several occasions when Jenny's mother, Noelene, was there but Norman wasn't, or vice versa. Or they'd be talking to their friends and other dog breeders. It was right on the tip of my tongue a couple of times but then we'd be interrupted or the conversation would lead in another direction. By the end of the day I was like a tightly wound pocket watch – time was ticking away and I wasn't getting anywhere. Finally I knew what my mates had been talking about.

There was no other choice but to try again. I told Jenny I'd had so much fun I'd decided to spend another day at the dog show. She couldn't believe it. Neither could her parents. The next day too drained away. It was already lunchtime and I was no closer to asking the big question. Was my second opportunity slipping through my fingers? Suddenly there was a pause in conversation. I sat there like a sheep hesitating at a gateway. Then I plunged on through, with a pounding heart and deep breath.

'I was wondering how you guys feel about me asking Jenny to marry me?' I said.

Noelene answered immediately. 'It's okay with me.'

Norman took a little longer. 'No ...' He paused. I couldn't believe my ears.

'... I don't ...' Another pause.

He's going to say no!

'... see anything wrong with it.'

Talk about giving me a heart attack. I'd have broken out in a cold sweat if I had been able to. If a moment ago I had been that sheep baulking in panic at the gateway, I'd just made the sanctuary of the mob. My relief was overwhelming, palpable. I could taste it, smell it, breathe it in.

The laconic Norman apologised profusely. He hadn't meant it to come out that way and we all laughed. Me loudest of all.

Until that day I'd occasionally wondered how Jenny's parents felt about me being in a wheelchair. I know it was something that worried my father. He said he tried to imagine himself in their shoes. He said, 'If Kate came home and said, "I'm going to marry this bloke in a wheelchair", you'd have some second thoughts, wouldn't you? I just hoped Jenny's parents were okay about it. I wondered what they thought.'

But the Blacks say they had no reservations whatsoever. They were thrilled that we were going to become engaged because they knew how happy our relationship had made their daughter. According to Noelene, she wasn't at all surprised. She remembered when Jenny met me, how she rang home at the first opportunity to tell her about this 'wonderful person' she'd interviewed. 'I hope one day, Mum, you'll get the opportunity to meet him,' she had said.

Amazingly, Noelene suspected then that Jenny had special feelings for me. 'With that mother's instinct, I thought, Jen really likes this fellow … mothers know these things sometimes.'

In fact, Jenny often mentioned to her parents that she'd spoken to me and she'd inevitably end the conversation by saying how much she liked me, and her mother thought again there was something there. 'One Christmas after they met, Sam rang to wish Jenny a Merry Christmas and I answered the phone and spoke to him for while. As I called Jenny to come to the phone, I remember thinking … I've never met this fellow but I feel as though I've known him for years.'

So it seems my request for Jenny's hand in marriage wasn't such a big surprise for her parents, although the fact I asked was a shock. That made me feel particularly glad I had. And their answer was such a bloody relief. Although I must admit, I haven't been to a dog show since.

Once I had the green light from Jenny's parents I began organising my surprise. Each weekday morning the ABC did a brain teaser, where the breakfast presenter asked listeners a quiz question right after Jenny's rural report and people would phone in with the answer. Perhaps I could ring in with a question of my own. First I got in touch with the breakfast presenter, Bill Gleeson. He was immediately enthusiastic and thought my idea would work. We started planning it, speaking on the phone a number of times. Then Bill had to take sick leave. Disaster. One minute it was all coming together, the next it was all falling apart.

I was so disappointed I nearly gave up on the idea then and there. That weekend I packed a champagne bottle and couple of glasses in my suitcase. I was going down to Tamworth to help Jenny paint a room in her house. I thought, 'I'll send her out of the room and paint "Marry me?" on the wall.'

But fate, in the form of Marg Warden, stepped in. I happened to call in on her and Mike on my way to Jenny's place and told them how my well-laid plans had come unstuck. When I told them what I was going to do instead, Marg wouldn't have a bar of it. She couldn't see why my original plan wasn't still possible. 'Why not talk to the station manager, Jackie Bowmer, instead? Here, let me take the champagne bottle and glasses out of your suitcase while you think about it.'

The following week I rang Jackie. She was every bit as excited as Bill had been about my idea. We worked out a scheme and had it all sorted out when we hit another snag. Unexpectedly, Jenny was asked to do the *Country Hour*, which went to air between noon and 1pm. She was to do the statewide program from the Tamworth studio all of the following week, which meant she didn't have to start work until seven. She was so excited. I wasn't. Again my plans were thrown out the window.

I called Jackie urgently. Luckily, she didn't want to give up the idea either. We'd just have to figure out a way to get Jenny on the breakfast program. But how?

So the following week Jenny presented the *Country Hour*. Meanwhile, I'd told her I was off to Brisbane to catch up with friends. I didn't want her suspecting anything. In reality, on Thursday afternoon I drove to Tamworth. As I was driving into town I phoned Jenny on my mobile.

'Gidday, Jen.'

'Hi, Sam. How's Brisbane?'

'I had a great trip up … what's happening down there?'

'Oh, Sam, you wouldn't believe it. Just when I thought I was going to have the luxury of doing the *Country Hour* and no early starts, Jackie rang to say she's not feeling very well and could I go in and do the breakfast program in the morning. I can't believe it, although I must admit she did look off-colour today.'

I smiled to myself. Finally, things were falling into place. We chatted, and then I said, 'Look, Jen, I've got to go. My mates are waiting and we're about to go down to the pub. Catch you later.'

'Bye, Sam. See you tomorrow.'

I hung up. There I was sitting in my car just outside Tamworth and she was sure I was in Brisbane. I spent the night with Mike and Marg, and hardly slept at all. I couldn't wait to get to the studio the next morning.

By 6.30am I'd had breakfast and was on my way to the studio with Marg and her eldest son, Jeremy. Bill Gleeson and the news journalist John McFarlane met us at the front door – what a surprise, I didn't expect to see them. They helped me up a flight of stairs and whisked me into Jackie's office, a small distance away from the studio.

Jenny was having a shocker of a program. There had been a power surge overnight and the highly computerised, hi-tech studio was experiencing a few glitches. The fact Jenny had had less than twelve hours' notice – little time to prepare the program – probably wasn't helping either.

It was approaching the seven o'clock news bulletin and the final music track started going to air. Jenny had completely forgotten the brain teaser. Suddenly Bill ran into the studio waving a piece of paper. She looked up, surprised. Bill had been off sick all week with the flu. 'What are you doing here?' she asked.

He mumbled something about needing to do a few things before the weekend, then said, 'Don't forget the brain teaser.' And he handed her the piece of paper with the day's question. The music faded into Jenny's voice: 'Here's this morning's brain teaser. In which year did Australia bring home no gold medals from the Olympics? If you know the answer, give me a call after the news. It's news time now on ABC Radio New England Northwest, it's seven o'clock.'

Luckily Jenny didn't come out of the studio or she would have discovered an unexpected hive of activity. She was too busy preparing the music and community notices for the next segment of the breakfast program. At eleven past seven she went back on air, read the brain teaser again and the day's weather forecast. The phones started ringing.

Normally a producer answered the callers, typing names and towns of residence on a computer in the production suite, which also came up on the screen in the studio. But that day the computer wasn't working. Instead someone had to furiously write the information on a piece of paper and run it into the studio. I told Bill to give Jenny a false name for me. He ran into the studio and handed her the paper. It read, 'Line 1 – David from Manilla.'

Jenny hit the button for line 1. 'Hello, David from Manilla?' All she got was a busy tone.

'We seem to be having problems with our phone lines this morning as well. If I can get someone up for the brain teaser I will.' As she spoke she hit line 2, planning to put whoever it was straight to air. Busy. Each time Jenny hit a line it was the same. It was every radio broadcaster's nightmare – live radio at its worst. Jenny thought it was due to failing technology, but unbeknown to her, the staff were dumping the outside calls because she was meant to get me.

Meanwhile, I was sitting there listening to all this – the frantic activity and voices in the production suite yelling, 'Line 1, line 1, pick up line 1 … no, line 2, pick up line 2 …' Poor old Jenny was on air apologising, on the verge of abandoning the brain teaser completely, and I was thinking it wasn't going to happen. I was about to storm into the studio and yell, 'Marry me,' when finally my call got through.

'Hello, I think we've finally got David from Manilla back on the line …'

'Hello, Jenny Black, this is Sam Bailey from Croppa Creek.'

For a moment Jenny was completely stumped but then a small, surprised voice said, 'Hello, Sam.'

'Jenny, I've got absolutely no idea of the answer to your brain teaser this morning, but on New England Northwest radio I've got a brain teaser for you. Will you marry me and spend the rest of your life by my side?'

Silence. Giggle. Then she said, 'I can't believe this.' Giggle.

'Jen, I led you to believe I was going to be in Brisbane yesterday and today but in actual fact I'm making this call from the ABC office and here I have a big bunch of red roses, an ear tag with Sam on it and a bottle of that bubbly stuff. I was wondering if you'd like to join me.'

Still no reply, which was surprising because normally Jenny could talk under wet cement. But she just giggled and kept saying, 'I can't believe this … I can't believe this.'

'But first you've got to give me an answer to my question.'

Finally she replied. 'Yes, Sam. Yes, I'll marry you.'

She put on a music track and almost ran out of the studio. The first person she saw was a very hale and hearty Jackie. And then there was Bill, who was meant to be off sick, and John McFarlane, who was meant to be on the afternoon shift. 'You were all in on this!'

They hugged and congratulated her and then she ran to me. It was such a fantastic moment. We wrapped our arms around each other and kissed. And it was all captured on video. Completely by chance was a young guy doing work experience there that week and he brought in his video camera. He videoed the whole thing, which was pretty amazing. It was particularly lucky because in all the rush that morning Jenny had forgotten to put on the logger tape – which normally records everything that goes to air – so we hadn't managed to catch it on audio.

Then the most unexpected thing happened. The phone lines all lit up and the fax machine started going flat out. In fact, it ran out of paper, as dozens of listeners wrote to congratulate us. We were taking calls for three hours – it was overwhelming, mind-blowing.

I'd been ready for a couple of calls. I'd told my parents and Jenny's of my intentions and mentioned to a few friends I was going to talk to Jenny on the radio that morning. But I didn't anticipate such an outpouring of emotion, mostly from complete strangers. What I hadn't factored in was the power of radio.

One guy called and told Jenny, 'I've been listening to you for years. You don't know me but I feel like I know you and I just had to call and tell you, that's the best bit of radio I've ever heard.'

People seemed genuinely moved. Some − men included − even said my proposal brought tears to their eyes. To this day we still meet people who vividly remember it. We might be having a hamburger in a café at Narrabri and someone will recognise us, and reminisce about hearing the radio that morning.

It's obviously something that stuck in people's minds and even if they didn't hear it they might recall their mother or grandmother or friend saying, 'We heard a fantastic thing on the radio this morning.' One of those things you remember, like man walking on the moon. The response was humbling and unexpected.

Later I tried to put my finger on why it touched a nerve with people. Perhaps it was because a proposal was normally a private, yet very special moment in someone's life and they got to share ours that morning. Perhaps it was because people were relieved to hear something positive, a good news story. They normally tuned into the radio and heard about wars or murders or car accidents or some other chaos. That day people were lying in bed, getting ready to face the day and all of a sudden they heard something uplifting and happy.

Maybe it's because deep down inside most people are sentimental; and the male listeners responded as much as the women did. Many people thought it was romantic. Funny, I wasn't thinking about romance when I was planning it. I just wanted to do something different and memorable. Once I'd planted the seed, I was too busy trying to make it grow to think about anything else. I imagined I'd jump off the tractor, hop in the car, drive down to Tamworth, pop the question, have lunch with Jen and be back on the tractor that afternoon.

How wrong I was. Prime Television and the local newspaper, the *Northern Daily Leader*, wanted to do a story, and we ended up in Column 8 of the Sydney Morning Herald the next day. Jenny was supposed to be riding at a one-day event that weekend, but she never made it. It was far too extraordinary a time to want to rush away to other things.

After the proposal quite a few people said to me quite seriously, 'Sam, what were you going to do if she said no?' I had no qualms about that. I knew it would probably stump her, but I had been one hundred per cent sure she'd say yes.

I guess the really terrific thing about it was that some people knew I had had a car accident and was a quadriplegic and that threw a whole different light on it. They knew I'd been to hell and back, so I think it was a great uplifting moment for us all. My little trick worked, way beyond my wildest imaginings.

The time between becoming engaged and marriage was one of the most wonderful in my life. There were engagement parties, a buck's party and a chance to catch up with old friends I hadn't seen in quite a while. It was also exciting because we were making plans for our future together.

Jenny and I discussed the idea of moving into the old house at Pine Hills. It hadn't been lived in for eight years and had fallen into some disrepair, so we decided to go over to check it out. What a sight it must have been – the two of us, a wheelchair and our dogs – as we piled onto the four-wheel bike and headed off.

The house, built in 1916, had been quite grand in its early days with wide sweeping verandahs and large timber casement windows. But it was only a ghost of its former self. The gutters were hanging sadly, the verandah boards were rotting away and when I sat inside in my wheelchair, it rolled across the room all of its own accord. Part of the roof had blown off a small two-room building behind the house and its floor was covered in sheep droppings. A nearby timber car shed had completely collapsed. The once impressive garden was long since gone. Sheep and cattle had grazed most of the garden plants to the ground, and they'd been replaced by overgrown grass and weeds. It was going to need some serious repairs and maintenance.

When we got back it was lunchtime and Mum – who was keen to know the outcome of our visit – was in the kitchen preparing a salad. 'Hi, Libby, can I help?' said Jenny.

As the two of them chopped away, not a word passed Jenny's lips about our trip over to see the house at Pine Hills. Mum went on cutting up carrots on the chopping board, waiting. Finally it got the better of her. 'What did you think of the house?'

Jenny paused and then said in a rather offhand manner, 'Oh, I think I'd put a bulldozer through it.'

Mum saw red and started fuming. She found herself thinking, 'I don't know why I'm getting lunch for you … you little twerp.' She almost broke the chopping board as she finished cutting up the salad, she whacked the knife down so hard. 'I reckon it'd probably be just as easy to put a match to it …' Jenny added. But then the look on Mum's face got too much for her. She lost it completely, bursting into peals of laughter. 'I'm only joking ... I absolutely loved it!'

A few months later, when Jenny arrived the week before the wedding, I wasn't so sure how she felt about it. She had just driven down our driveway – five kilometres of partly blacksoil bush track – to deliver her final carload of goods and chattels. She walked onto the verandah and burst into tears. There she stood at the top of the back stairs, a pile of rocks and cement and rubble, with tears pouring down her face, sobbing her heart out.

Beside her on the verandah, where the local wildlife had regularly sheltered from the weather, lay a scattering of roo droppings. Before her stood her new home. By then basic repairs were done. The building had been restumped, verandah boards had been replaced, the kitchen and bathrooms given a basic overhaul and new gutters now meant the rainwater tank might actually catch some runoff.

There was no doubting its potential, but at that stage it was still a long way from being a home. A daunting cleaning and renovation job lay ahead. Hornets' nests snuggled into the corners of the rooms and cobwebs hung like dusty curtains from the ceilings. The windows were covered in dirty skid marks where birds had been throwing themselves at their own reflections in the glass. Jenny's belongings were in pieces or packed in boxes, scattered throughout the house, delivered hastily a couple of weeks earlier.

Since then she'd been sleeping in her swag and eating out of an esky while she finished painting her house at Tamworth ready for tenants. She had been wielding a paintbrush from dawn until well after dark for days. Add the stress of organising a wedding and it was a fatal mix.

She'd also had to say a few goodbyes. A month earlier she'd farewelled her loyal ABC listeners in an emotional final program. While I don't think she fully appreciated it at the time, it was a big step giving up her career to move to Croppa Creek to marry me. She was leaving behind a high-profile job that in her mind defined who she was. That was something she didn't even recognise herself for a long time, but eventually she was able to put that image of herself behind her and find a new sense of who she was.

Not only was she leaving her job, career and house behind, she was also moving away from her friends in Tamworth and further away from her family at Scone. While getting married was an incredibly joyous, wonderful time, it was also a time of grieving – which Jenny, like most people, didn't realise. She said about her crying, 'I don't think I was unhappy … it was just the symptom of being on an emotional rollercoaster. I was really excited about it as well. It was exciting to go and do something different and start a whole new life. It was exciting to be with Sam.'

On 20 March 1999 Jenny and I were married in The Armidale School chapel. I didn't have any of the nerves many people say they have. I couldn't wait to get to the church, see Jenny and become her husband. As I waited at the front of the chapel, I felt an overwhelming sense of amazement – disbelief that I was really there waiting for my bride. It seemed surreal that all those people behind me in the pews were there to watch us exchange vows. So many times I'd sat among the congregation and witnessed the wedding of other people, never believing it would ever happen to me. I sat there with four of my best mates and my brother beside me and felt like one of the pack again, surrounded by friends – many who'd sat with the fit, young, physical me in that same chapel throughout my school years. At that moment, it no longer mattered that I was in a wheelchair.

As Jenny walked down the aisle, I made a funny face at her – it was my way of expressing my joy and absolute happiness to her. I wanted to laugh and cry and fly all at the same time.

We turned to face the minister, Reverend Bill Howarth, whom we'd especially invited back for the occasion. Formerly my school chaplain, he'd conducted the eerie prayer service in that very same building all those years before, the night I could have died.

And so the man and the chapel completed the circle. They were the link between the lowest and highest points in my journey as a quadriplegic. It seemed appropriate that it was so.

'Do you, Sam Alexander Bailey, take Jennifer Maree Black to be your lawful, wedded wife?'

I shouted out 'I do!' so loudly it echoed around the rafters. It erupted, exploded from my mouth, propelled by all the love for Jenny I felt inside me. Perhaps, in a way, I was yelling it from my mountaintop. Everyone roared with laughter.

Later Mum and Dad said that moment would stay with them forever. After a twelve-year rollercoaster ride from the depths of despair, to soaring achievements and everything in between, they thought this was by far the highest point – the day they knew their eldest son had finally found true, uninhibited happiness.

For me, my favourite moment was when I took Jenny's hand after she'd walked up the aisle. I knew than, metaphorically, that I'd never have to let it go. In the weeks leading up to our wedding we'd talked about how wonderful it was going to be not to have to say goodbye ever again. I hated it when I was visiting Jenny in Tamworth and on Sunday afternoons I had to leave.

These days most people live together before they marry – they call it try before you buy – but we never did. Obviously in my situation it was pretty much impossible because I lived with my parents, but I wouldn't have done it anyway. I think not living together was a bonus because the wedding wasn't only about having a party and signing a document, it was the beginning of a whole new life for both of us. Now we had our whole lives ahead of us to get to know each other. I couldn't wait to learn the little things, like how Jenny put the toothpaste on her toothbrush, how she brushed her hair, her likes and dislikes. It was the mundane, everyday things that I looked forward to sharing.

But our marriage ceremony meant much more than that even. It changed my life and gave me an independence and freedom to pursue my own dreams in a way that had never before been possible. It opened another gateway and led me down a new and unexpected path.

TWELVE

MY LITTLE MATE

I can't express how it felt to drive into Pine Hills for the first time with my little mate tucked under my arm. I've talked about finding my legs and becoming productive again and climbing my own personal Mount Kosciusko but nothing compared to this. This was Mount Everest in comparison – all my dreams come true.

Finding Jenny meant I had someone to share my life. Two halves making a whole. But it also transformed the way I lived. She made a difference with the small things. Now when I went to town, I didn't have to yell out to a complete stranger to help get my chair out and hope like hell he didn't run a mile. If I was in a shop and bought something, I didn't have to ask someone to take it out to the car and to hang around while I got in, then load my chair. Over the years I'd become reasonably comfortable with that, but in my eyes it still took away some of my masculinity. I had been constantly putting myself out on a limb, vulnerable to the mixed reactions I got from people.

Marriage to Jenny also meant big things in my life would never be the same. Now I had company when I travelled and someone to go on holidays with. She was there to share the experiences and reminiscence with afterwards.

She made my life much easier on the farm as well, helping with the little jobs that cropped up. In fact, she's become a regular Mrs Fix-It. She changes the blades on my slasher, fills up my spray rig, fixes leaking troughs or strains loose fences. Mum and Dad were always happy and willing to help, but I hated asking them all the time. Now I didn't have to.

And Jenny is a country girl at heart, practical and willing to have a go at anything. I think that had a lot to do with why I was so attracted to her. From our first few weeks together and visiting her Tamworth home, I quickly realised she was very much an outdoor person. You can't choose the one you fall in love with, but it meant a lot to me, in the position I was in, to be with someone who didn't mind getting her hands dirty. It would have been quite difficult if I'd married a girl who tended to squawk if she got a bit of shit or dirt on her. That would have made my life even more frustrating. Not that I would have fallen for someone like that anyway. Jenny was perfect for me in every way and that's what I loved about her. If someone had told me I would find a great match, I couldn't have believed in my wildest dreams she could be quite so ideal. She was the ball to my socket, the nut to my bolt. She fitted perfectly.

Thanks to Jenny many new doors opened for me. I'd never gone shopping just for pleasure before. It was a real novelty to buy groceries, for example. I relished wandering down the aisles, hunting around and seeing what was on the shelves. I liked the togetherness of it and discovering we both loved bookshops and hardware stores. We'd wander in them for hours.

With Jenny by my side I discovered a new sense of independence. Now I could dine out at a restaurant whenever I felt like it. Previously I had never done that unless I was catching up with mates. I felt like part of the gang again – I could go to a dinner or lunch or party and there were two of us. Before that I'd always gone alone and felt like Terry-tag-along.

There was also a tremendous sense of relief to be moving away from Mum and Dad. Even though we all loved and respected one another, I hated the fact I was in my thirties and still living with 'Mummy and Daddy'. It wasn't easy for anyone concerned. I felt I was interfering in their personal life, taking away their privacy. They deserved to be Darby and Joan, like all their friends.

On that topic Mum said, 'Apart from all the care Sam needed, there were certain disruptions to our lives. I felt I had to feed him well, so I had to make an effort to have meat and three vegies for dinner and salads for lunch and extra things he might need.

'The three of us would sit down to watch television with Sam's wheelchair right up in the middle so he could see everything. And he wasn't terribly inclined to watch *Pride and Prejudice* or *Brideshead Revisited*. He'd say, 'What are you watching this crap for?' and he'd flick it over to something dreadful and we'd go to bed.'

Mum was so right. Now they could live their lives the way they wanted to, and so could I.

Finally I was king of my own castle, and I got so much joy out of that. It was fun deciding what colour to paint a room, stripping, sanding and putting it all back together just the way we wanted it. As I've already mentioned, the house was still in need of a lot of tender loving care when we first got married. Aside from the cleaning and painting – it hadn't seen a paintbrush in years – it wasn't very accessible. The builders had made me a ramp up onto the western verandah but it was too steep. Then there was a trek across the lawn and a bit further to get to the car shed and my ute. We had a few tools but they were stacked on the floor. We didn't have any storage or shelves or anything in the shed – it was an empty shell. The house yard was a jungle, overgrown with grass, with holes in the ground and wheel tracks where the builders had come and gone.

Two days after our wedding we arrived home and had to find the jigsaw pieces of our bed and put it together. It was an ancient double brass bed Jenny had been given by her grandfather. It looked immediately at home in our old house as it was a little the worse for wear, having been carted around the countryside as Jenny moved from place to place in her career as a journalist. We eventually found some sheets, blankets and pillows. At least now we had a bed to sleep on, among the rubble of our possessions. I probably should say Jenny's possessions, because I owned virtually only my clothes and a couple of old pieces of furniture.

Setting up house was a bit of an adventure, reminding me of the stories of how my own parents started out. They began their married life on Bardin, which Dad owned in partnership with a mate. The deal was that whoever married first had to move out of the main house. It turned out to be Dad. So he and Mum dragged the original Bardin schoolhouse up onto the top of a hill, a few kilometres away. They started with this two-room building on a rocky hill in among the cypress pines, belahs and kurrajong trees. It had spectacular views, but it must have been a daunting task for the new bride. While Mum grew up in Warialda, she'd been living in London during her twenties and enjoying the high life. But she attacked the house and surrounds with relish. When I was two and they moved back down to the main Bardin house, she left behind her first beautiful garden. She had to start all over again. It always amazed me how hard my parents did it. I was glad I was following in their footsteps in a sense. Mind you, I didn't have it nearly as tough as they did – they even had a pit loo.

On no account did I want to waltz into Mum and Dad's house at Bardin with the pool and tennis court and everything a going concern – achievements which had taken them almost a lifetime to build. I wanted to save and work and do it my way, and then I'd value every little improvement. Not that I had much choice. Jenny and I didn't have the money to go full bore, to do a major renovation. Instead, we did it room by room, acre by acre – with occasional help from friends and family when they came to visit. For us it was all about cleaning and scrubbing and mowing and planting trees and turning nothing into something special. It all brought a great sense of accomplishment and was made all that much better because I was doing it with my best mate.

Jenny didn't mind living in the middle of nowhere, in a house that was a mess when we were first married. Some girls would have taken one look and run a mile, but Jenny didn't. She just got in and cleaned it up.

Our home is still a work in progress. The only bathroom we have is on the opposite end of the house to our bedroom and outside as well. So it's quite an expedition to get to the bathroom and a cold streak in the middle of winter. But I don't dwell on it. That's just the way it is and I just do it. It's not going to kill me. Eventually we'll have the luxury of an inside bathroom and we'll really appreciate it when we can duck through a doorway into the shower and loo, where it's warm in winter and cool in summer.

When we first got married we had no cooling and very little heating. We had an electric oil heater for our bedroom, but apart from that the only heating we had was a little fan heater Jenny had brought with her. It didn't have much impact in the huge rooms in our house which stretch five by five metres across, with ceilings over three metres high. And it was made much worse by the two- or three-centimetre gaps under the doors, the crevices around the windows and the cold air rising up through the floorboards.

We were married in March and a couple of months later temperatures plummeted. One day we were so cold we were turning blue. It was one of those days when the wind goes straight through you. We sat eating lunch in the kitchen, still wrapped in our overcoats. We looked at each other and said almost in unison, 'Let's get the fire going.'

There was an old wood heater in a brick fireplace in the lounge room which we'd partly dismantled, intending to throw it out. We thought it wasn't any good because it was rusty and full of water, but that day we were desperate. It took a hammer and WD40 to force the door open, revealing a firebox that was red with decaying steel, glistening in a pool of stagnant water. We mopped it up, scraped away the rust and tried to light the fire. It took a few attempts but finally it spluttered into life and we huddled around it – drawn like cockatoos to a grain silo. Later we discovered it needed only a new top on the flue and we're still warming ourselves around it today. In fact, it's a cracker of a fireplace.

It was fun to discover how similar our tastes were. We both like antiques and wood, things that are natural and rustic. No laminex and plastic for us.

Before I was married I did most of the mustering myself. We only had one bike and some of the paddocks were too rough and inaccessible for Dad's Toyota, so I had to do a lot of it alone. Some paddocks were more difficult than others – along Croppa Creek was a nightmare because there weren't many places where I could cross. I'd be going backwards and forwards from one side to the other trying to hunt the cattle out. It was painfully slow and invariably there'd be a few cattle I couldn't get. So mustering was often a long, drawn-out affair that was as frustrating as keeping a rogue cow out of a barley crop.

Then Jenny came along on a horse and made it so much easier. She could fly down through the creek after the cattle and wheel them back. Between the two of us, with a two-way radio each to communicate, the mustering became a cinch. My frustrations were replaced with enjoyment, multiplied by the fact that Jenny got a lot of fun out of it. She was passionate about horses and loved nothing more than mustering in the creek with the wind through her hair, a regular jillaroo. Having grown up on a sheep and cattle place herself, she was immediately at home in both the paddock and the cattle yards.

And there was another bonus to having Jen mustering with me – she was there to rescue me when I threatened to slip off the bike. I'd yell out, she'd canter over on her horse and push me back on – my personal guardian angel.

Even so, she wasn't always there to help, at least not on cue. One day I headed off to set up some gates while Jenny saddled her horse and she was going to catch up. I pulled up beside a gate, undid the latch and pushed it open. At the time the accelerator on my bike would sometimes stick but I was used to it, and knew to be careful. That morning, I went to putt off and the accelerator stuck. The front wheel climbed the mesh of the gate, like a goanna up a tree trunk, tipping the bike onto its side. I came off fairly gracefully and was unhurt. I bummed my way around to the side where the seat was and rested my back against the padding to wait for Jenny, knowing she'd be along soon on her horse.

Shortly afterwards I heard this almighty scream, 'Sam ... Sam are you okay ... Sam?' and the sound of hooves galloping towards the bike. I saw a glimpse of Jenny's face pale and tight with terror, then flushed with relief.

'Sam, you frightened me. I thought you were under the bike ...' she was shaking and angry and very upset.

'I'll never forget that morning,' said Jenny. 'I was riding towards the gateway when I saw the bike. Initially I thought it was upside down ... and I couldn't quite figure it out. Then I realised I was looking at its underbelly and wheels. But I couldn't see Sam. I kicked my horse into a gallop and as I got closer, all I could see were Sam's legs sticking out from behind the bike. I thought his body was underneath it. I'll never forget how I felt. I felt sick, like my whole world had suddenly caved in on me. In fact, when I think back I can't actually go there – because the overwhelming fear I felt is not a place I wish to go again. When I realised Sam was okay, I was really angry with him. At the time I don't think he could understand my reaction, but I thought he was dead. After a lot of heaving I managed to get the bike back on its wheels and helped Sam back on. I'd been so frightened, and then so relieved that as we rode down the road to the paddock we were mustering I burst into tears.'

It didn't occur to me that I would scare Jenny. I was sitting there, leaning against the bike with a big smile on my face and thinking, 'Things didn't go quite to plan this morning.'

One afternoon on my way back from Mum and Dad's I saw a bull in the wrong paddock. That night I mentioned to Jenny – who was riding out the next morning to check some cows – 'If you happen to see him you might just run him back into the paddock.' But next morning as I headed back to Bardin, he was near the gate and I thought, 'While I'm here I'll just duck him through. Piece of cake.' But he'd obviously had a rugged time with the other bulls in his rightful paddock and wasn't keen to go back. I chased him around and around a couple of times, but he wasn't going to have a bar of it. Eventually I became so frustrated I rammed his backside with the front of the bike. He didn't like that much but it made me feel better. Then we weren't far from the gate so I stopped. Tooting the horn and yelling like an overzealous footy fan, I waited for him to walk through.

He had other ideas. He turned his beady eyes towards me, dropped his head and charged. Here was this huge black bull, almost a tonne of powerful, angry muscle and bone closing in on me. As he got nearer the ground reverberated under his approaching hooves. I sat there hoping like hell he'd only shunt the bike back a bit. 'As long as I hang on,' I thought, 'I'll be all right.'

I totally underestimated him. I couldn't believe the force as his skull slammed into the bullbar, bending the two-inch steel pipe.

Then he lifted – that's why they call rising share prices a 'bull market'. I was witnessing a rise of astronomical proportions. He flung the bike backwards as if it was weightless, tossing me off the back like confetti. As I landed with a thump on the hard grey dirt, I had visions of three hundred kilos of metal bike crashing down on top of me.

Fortune was smiling on me that day, and the bike bounced, like a cat, back onto its four wheels. But the bull wasn't finished. He came looking for me. Snorting and furious, he investigated his handiwork. I'm not sure if he pushed me or not. It all happened so quickly. Then, obviously satisfied I wouldn't be disturbing him again, he trotted off down the fence – in the opposite direction to the gateway, of course.

Gingerly I checked to see if I was okay. With relief, I thought I was. So I bummed my way around beside the bike and climbed back on. I'd been heading for Bardin to do a couple of jobs, so I did that, then went home. By then I was feeling a bit off colour, but thought, 'I'm just battered and bruised. Like I've done a couple of rounds with Mike Tyson. I'll be all right.'

When Jenny arrived home I was sitting on the verandah. When I told her what had happened, she wasn't surprised. She was worried I'd been hurt in my tussle with the bull that day, but I was positive I was okay.

By the next day I wasn't so sure. I had a slight headache and felt I wasn't sitting right. Off to the doctor we went and he sent me to have x-rays. The radiologist made the remark, 'Thank God you're in the position you're in, because if you could feel pain like a normal person you'd be in agony. Your pelvis is fractured in three places.'

Four long and boring weeks in bed followed. It was bloody frustrating because I couldn't do anything. Once I'd read *The Land and Farm Machinery Deals* from cover to cover, I'd resort to *Women's Weekly* and when I was really desperate, one of Jenny's horse magazines. I caught up with the latest on *Days of Our Lives*, *The Young and the Restless* and *The Bold and the Beautiful*, using a long stick to change the channels because our TV was too old for a remote.

My stint in bed took me back to my early weeks in the spinal unit – not a pleasant reminder. But I survived and I've never been so glad to feel the sun on my face and wind in my hair as I was when I got back on the bike again.

Our house is tucked away pretty well from the closest public road – as I've mentioned before, it's five kilometres by predominantly blacksoil track. There are four small gullies plus Croppa Creek to cross. In the early days, when we only had my ute, twenty millimetres of rain was enough to turn the black soil into a slippery, boggy mess.

Later we progressed to a four-wheel drive, which meant we could churn in or out, but most of the time we preferred not to because it just damaged the road. Instead we often had rushed trips home trying to beat the rain.

One Saturday night we were at the Warialda Show. It's always a great event because everyone comes out of the woodwork. We were having a ball, catching up with all our mates, taking very little notice of the light rain falling. But that quickly changed when the secretary came over to report that Mum was on the phone. We'd better leave, it was pouring down at home.

We had a forty-minute trip ahead of us, and about halfway we hit the rain. It bucketed down virtually the rest of the way home. It was coming down in sheets, leaving grey blankets of water across the roadway which shone in the headlights. We were in the ute, so we knew we couldn't get to our house. Instead we went to Mum and Dad's.

We could have stayed with them I guess, but we had animals to feed, so we thought we'd brave the journey in the wet. After all, it was a bit of an adventure. The only option was the four-wheel bike – by now Mum and Dad had one at their place too. They gave us raincoats. We strapped the wheelchair frame on the front, tied the wheels on the back and headed into the dark, pouring rain. What a bizarre sight it would have been – the wheelchair precariously balanced on the front, me trying to peer around it to see where I was going and Jenny hiding behind me trying to avoid the flying mud as much as possible.

It took us half an hour to get home. By the time we pulled into the sanctuary of our garage we were splattered from head to toe with black lumps of mud, many looking like they had tails formed by rivulets of water and dirt flowing down our faces and raincoats. We were like drowned rats. But we were warm inside and laughing so hard we were almost falling off the bike at the thought of how we must have looked.

Another time we got caught out when we'd been shopping, so we rode home on the bike with the esky tied on the back and bags of groceries hanging off the handlebars, plus the wheelchair. Sometimes these trips also included two or three dogs, all piled on top of each other and of course, the wheelchair. It was a real hillbilly turnout.

Rather than risk getting bogged in the car in the rain, we'd usually opt for the bike, but there were times when we'd chance it, which made Jenny very nervous. Jenny explains: 'I always dreaded us getting bogged because I knew I'd be the one who would have to traipse home through the mud and slush, probably in my best shoes, to get Sam's bike. And of course, by the time I'd retrieved him and his chair – and they'd both been dragged and pushed from the car to the bike – there would have been mud and water everywhere. I have visions of washing Sam down under the hose, because there's no way I'd be letting him and his chair into the house covered in mud. Thankfully, so far it hasn't happened.'

The access was all part of the fun and excitement of living in the bush. If Jenny had been a prima donna she probably wouldn't have been happy on the back of the bike getting sprayed in mud and manure, or in the cattle yards covered in dust and flies. As it was, she took it in her stride.

There is one thing Jenny doesn't like about our life. That's the possibility of me coming off the bike. She says, 'I sometimes wonder when Sam speeds off if I'll see him again, especially after being involved in some of his little episodes. I worry about losing Sam but then I think, just be thankful for every day I have with him and hope like hell it doesn't happen. He assures me he's much tamer now than he used to be, so goodness knows what he was like before.'

It's true that I am a lot more careful now I've got Jenny. It would devastate me if something happened to her, so I think she'd feel the same way if something happened to me. Before it didn't seem to matter as much – while obviously my family would be sad, it's not the same as losing your soulmate.

Now I don't take the same risks when I'm in the creek. Like the other day, I thought about going across Croppa Creek when it was in flood. The water was about a metre deep. I wanted to check some cattle on the other side. Normally I would have had a go, but I thought, 'No, if you don't get across and you get washed away and drown, what about Jenny?' So I take it a lot easier now. It's probably an age thing too. I'm starting to feel the wear and tear on my body.

It doesn't mean things don't still happen. One day I was starting the pump. I'd worked out how I could back the bike up to the pump, fill it with fuel and pull start the engine. I'd swing my leg over the fuel tank of the bike and twist around, lying belly down on the back. This particular morning as I swung my leg back over the centre – the toe of my boot hit the accelerator and again it stuck. The bike took off like a bolting horse, throwing me onto the ground, and just kept going. It climbed up and over a ringlock fence – how it managed to do that without tipping over, I'll never know – plunging across the road, down a gully and finally came to a halt, motor running, out of my sight. It was at least sixty metres away, which may as well have been the other side of the Sydney Harbour as far as I was concerned. What was I going to do?

Jenny was waiting for me at home and I was worried that if she came searching for me, she wouldn't see me beside the pump. I was surrounded by huge variegated thistles, which towered over my head. 'Shit,' I thought, 'I'll have to get out onto the road.' It was about twenty metres away. I found an old bit of pipe, about half the length of a broomstick, and set to the thistles like a man possessed. It certainly helped ease some of the frustration. I'd swipe a bit, bum my way forwards through the thorns and spikes, then swipe again, bum forwards, until I made it to the fence, my bare hands and arms a mass of red spots from the prickles. I forced up the netting, dragging myself underneath. Eventually I made it to the road, battered and grazed and a little worse for wear, but I made it.

I could hear Jenny calling over the two-way on the bike, 'Sam, are you on channel? Are you on channel, Sam?' A while later she drove down the road. It was a hell of a relief – it would have been a long way bumming my way to the bike. But I would have done it if I'd had to.

It would have been mind-boggling for Jenny to see me sitting on the road and the bike all the way down in the gully. She didn't disagree: 'I saw Sam in the distance, sitting on the road, and then as I got closer I noticed the bike. I couldn't for the life of me figure out how he'd ended up where he was and the bike all that distance away, on its wheels and still running.'

You'll be pleased to know that after that incident, I finally got the accelerator on the bike fixed.

Then there was the time we both went down to fix a flood fence. Jenny was too short to reach the top of the iron post to hammer it in. So I'd reversed up to the post and she'd stood on the back of the bike. We'd done that many, many times. Jenny would hit one steel post in and then we'd move onto the next one. We made quite a team.

On this occasion the post was in the sandy bottom of Croppa Creek and the bike was on a slope. Jenny was hammering the post in with a rock. I turned around on the bike to watch and thought I'd pinch Jenny's bum, as you do. But as I reached around with my hand I lost my balance and fell forward onto the accelerator. The bike was in reverse and leapt into life, bucking Jenny off the side as it catapulted over the iron post. It was in sand so it didn't provide much resistance. The bike kept going backwards into a shallow waterhole surrounded by low bottlebrush trees.

Jenny said, 'I'll never forget the sight of Sam and the bike lurching back into the branches of the bottle trees. He looked like he was going to get swallowed up. I wondered when he was going to stop and if he'd be okay when he did. I must admit, it sent me into a panic – it's much worse to be watching than experiencing it yourself. Sam was too busy just hanging on.'

The bike eventually tipped on the sloping ground and came to a spluttering halt on its side, depositing me in the muddy bog hole, one leg caught underneath. I wasn't hurt and Jenny helped me crawl out. I was covered from head to toe down one side in sticky, smelly goo – like a pig in mud. What a sight.

The big dilemma then was how to get the bike back on its wheels. It wasn't possible for Jenny to lift it by herself. And time was running out because it was late afternoon and would soon be dark. I told Jenny to race back to the house and get some rope, wire and the wire strainers. There was a tree trunk just above the bike, which we could use to lever the bike back up onto its wheels. Jenny took off up the steep creek bank like a hare with a dog on its tail.

She recalled, 'And as I was going up over the bank I heard Sam yell out after me, 'And bring back the camera. This might be one for the book.' I'd just watched Sam almost kill himself and there he was telling me to take photographs!'

Jenny ran most of the two or three kilometres home, loaded up the car and was back in under half an hour. She winched the bike back onto its wheels. Miraculously it was relatively unscathed, with only a couple of small scratches and looking like it had been given a muddy paint job on one side. I climbed back on it and amazingly it started. We fixed the fence and made it home shortly before dark.

I've never lost the feeling of helplessness I get when I come off my bike or out of my chair. When I'm lying on the floor or ground and it's such a struggle just to sit up, it's a powerful reminder of how incapacitated I really am. Sometimes I forget, especially if I haven't had a buster for a while. But it all comes flooding home to me when I'm trying to lift eighty kilos of virtually dead weight back up onto my bike or into my chair.

Another thing I've never got used to is Jenny going away. I miss her desperately and feel terribly lonely, even if she's away for only one day. Like an apple without its core. In fact, as soon as she leaves I can't wait for her to return, and when she's back, I appreciate her even more.

It's not so much that I can't survive for a few days on my own. I can. But occasionally something goes pear-shaped, like it did the very first time Jenny went away after we were married. We were still sleeping in Jenny's old brass bed and one night I went to transfer onto it and the whole timber base under the mattress dropped through the frame. My legs flew up in the air and I fell backwards down the steep slope formed by the mattress. I lay there like a see-saw, with my head at the lower end and my feet at the top. After quite a struggle, I eventually rolled my whole body down to the bottom and crawled, painstakingly, under the rectangular frame of the bed. I had no alternative; I couldn't get over the top.

Twenty long minutes later I was finally free and thought, 'What am I going to do now?' With a fair bit of heaving I managed to drag the mattress under the frame behind me and away from the bed. It was such a drama, but I didn't have any choice. There weren't any other beds set up in the house at that stage and I was very aware of the threat of pressure sores, so I couldn't just curl up on the carpet. I grabbed the doona, got on the mattress and went to sleep.

Next morning I had to bum my way over to the bed to grab my clothes, then back to the mattress to get dressed, then back to the bed to climb into my chair. I was very pleased when Jenny arrived back home, I can tell you.

A couple of times I have also fallen off my bath bench when Jenny wasn't here, and one night I flipped myself in my wheelchair while in the bathroom, getting my feet caught under the lip of the hand basin. I was stuck. That one had me worried there for a while, but I eventually managed to wriggle around enough to get my feet free.

Jenny worries when she goes away: 'I think the pressure is probably felt more by the people around Sam, like me and his parents. We never quite stop wondering if he is okay and every night I call just to make sure.'

Jenny and I have been married now for more than seven years. And I fall more in love with her every day. No one ever told me that happens. She's made me so happy because I've found my best mate and we are made for each other. It's such an amazing thing to find your soulmate and spend virtually every minute together, to share similar passions and have so much in common. Sometimes I ask myself, 'What if I'd never found her?' I imagine what my life would have been like and what I'd have missed out on. It scares me. But of course, if I hadn't met Jenny, I would never have known how good life could be.

I probably appreciate our relationship more than most couples do because I waited so long and thought it would never happen. And Jenny has made such a huge difference to my life because I'm disabled. But I also believe in being grateful. Sometimes you've got to sit and smell the flowers and I don't think a lot of people do. They tear through life and don't put a lot of value on where they live, their wife, husband or kids. They don't value the fact they have clean drinking water, food on the table, can watch the sun come up in the morning and walk free on the streets.

The only regret I have is that I didn't find Jenny ten years earlier.

THIRTEEN

OPENING ANOTHER GATE

Building a relationship with Jenny didn't simply change my life, it added a whole extra dimension to my story. No longer is it just about a bloke suffering an injury and getting his life back on track. Now it is also a tale of romance and, as my very public marriage proposal proved, scratch anyone's skin and underneath you'll find a romantic.

It was that extra dimension that helped open a new gateway and led me down an unexpected path. The gate began opening after a great friend and freelance journalist, Amanda Ducker, approached us about writing up our story for a magazine. We agreed and the article was published in August 1999, in the *Australian Women's Weekly*. A few months later the phone rang.

'This is Caitlin Shea, a producer with *Australian Story* ...'

She wanted to do my story? It was like having a national selector ringing to say I'd been chosen to play cricket or rugby for Australia – unbelievable. Caitlin made the call at the suggestion of Deb

Fleming, the program's executive producer. Deb said, 'At that stage we had a two- or three-story format, very different from now … we had a slot for a shorter piece … I was glancing through the women's magazines, as you do, and came across Sam's story. I thought, "That sounds really charming and it's a rural setting … that could make a nice piece."'

That was what had prompted the call. But it wasn't an easy decision for me. Jenny and I were avid fans of *Australian Story*, which broadcast weekly on ABC television. We thought the stories were well put together and inspiring. But I was reluctant to say yes because I didn't think my story was good enough. It was Jenny who finally talked me into it.

A few weeks later the crew arrived from Brisbane. It included Caitlin as the producer, cameraman Anthony Sines and sound recordist Marc Smith. We were lucky they arrived at all after an eventful trip down. They managed to get lost at one stage, ran over a feral pig and nearly had a head-on with a truck. Anthony said, 'We were yakking away like we always do and suddenly we came around a corner and there was a road train coming towards us on the wrong side of the road.' Thankfully they eventually made it to Pine Hills, no doubt wondering what they were going to find at the end of our long and winding entrance road.

Initially the plan was for Caitlin to stay with us, while Anthony and Marc would find accommodation in Warialda 'because they like to get away from the story at night', Caitlin told us. But they took one look, fell in love with the place and decided to stay as well.

Most of our filming took place in the early morning and late afternoon light. From the word 'go' it was different to any interviews I'd ever done before. Caitlin didn't want to know only about my accident, she wanted to know how I felt. She got right under my skin, like an itch that I just had to scratch. It brought out a lot of emotion. In a way she was rewinding the clock, making me reveal more than I ever had before. That was daunting, especially when I was in front of a camera for the first time. But the comforting thing was knowing I'd seen other *Australian Stories* and they'd been done very well.

While it was confronting, it was also fascinating filming the program. For the first time I realised how long it took to shoot such a small amount of air time. We'd shoot a scene but the wind would be blowing my hair the wrong way, so we'd shoot it again. Then the dog would bark at exactly the wrong time. We'd do it again. It was also interesting to see how they use lights and coloured paper on the windows in the background and things like that to create the mood and atmosphere.

In between filming, we ate, drank, talked, laughed a lot and had a great time. By the time the ABC team departed, we'd made some new friends, but we were left wondering how in the world they were going to jam all that footage into a story of only eight minutes.

The answer wasn't what we expected. After the editor, Roger Carter, saw the footage and interviews, he decided the story deserved a longer piece. The fact that we had footage of my marriage proposal to Jenny live on ABC radio was extra incentive. But they needed to shoot some more. Deb and Roger insisted on some footage of me flying an ultralight – they thought it was vital to the story. But my aircraft was well and truly out of action by then; it hadn't been up in the air for years.

So we tracked down a suitable ultralight at Boonah in Queensland and filmed the flying there. I'll never forget the lengths Anthony went to to get a good shot. He strapped the camera – a huge, broadcast-quality camera worth more than $100,000 – onto one of the wing struts. 'It was insane,' he admits now. 'You wouldn't normally risk a camera like that; the ABC's pretty particular about that sort of thing.' And Deb added, '… let alone if it had dropped on someone's head.' But he got some stunning shots and within a couple of months, 'Something in the Air' was ready for broadcast.

It was pretty scary sitting down to watch the piece for the first time in February 2000. We didn't know what it would be like. But our apprehension quickly turned to relief and then delight. We were amazed at how beautifully it was put together, how well they told the story.

For me it was also strange. It was like seeing my photo in a newspaper for the first time, finding myself surprised that I'd done something to deserve a mention. And there was the feeling of curiosity, wondering how I looked when I transferred onto my bike or when I was riding it. It was certainly an eye-opener for me. I saw my whole life from a completely different perspective.

It looked a lot easier than it felt. I knew how hard I had to concentrate — to maintain my balance, think through the whole process every time I got on the bike – making sure that house of cards didn't fall. But when I watched it on television, it looked like I sidled casually up in my chair and climbed on, with hardly a conscious thought.

Our story lasted fifteen minutes and the moment it finished, the phone rang and rang and rang. In the end we had to take the handpiece off the hook so we could take part in the internet forum after the program, as we'd agreed to do.

The web response was overwhelming too. People I hadn't seen in years got in touch – a bloke I'd played footy with fifteen years earlier, schoolmates I hadn't had contact with since leaving TAS, friends from the Northern Territory, even Bruce McMullen, who'd taught me to fly. There were also dozens of others who were complete strangers, some who were wheelies but most who weren't. People who were moved enough by my story to want to comment or ask questions.

Then when the forum was over, we put the phone back on the hook and it began ringing again. Over the next few days some of the calls or emails were from people wanting me to speak at various functions. I'd stumbled upon a new and unexpected calling – as a public speaker. Not that my rise to the lectern surprised my family. I come from a long line of natural orators. My mother's father, Don McGregor, had been the local stock agent, auctioneer and the most sought-after master of ceremonies in Warialda and district. On my father's side, most of Dad's five brothers loved nothing more than to get up and tell a yarn or two. And so speaking, for me, came naturally.

At first I spoke at functions for Rotary and schools and at local fundraisers, that sort of thing. Either the organisers contacted me via *Australian Story* or they knew me or of me through someone else. It started simply but with time snowballed. And I have *Australian Story* to thank because I suspect it might not have happened otherwise. It provided the launching pad.

A couple of nights after *Australian Story* went to air a woman rang from Serpentine, south of Perth in Western Australia. She introduced herself as Judy Hambley and said she was calling because a great friend of hers had recently suffered a spinal injury in a horse riding accident and was in the Perth spinal unit doing it tough. Would I write to her?

'Don't be silly,' I said. 'Give me her phone number and I'll ring her.'

And so began a friendship with Maria Archer, her family and friends. Over the next few months I kept in touch, sharing my experiences in the spinal unit and trying to convince Maria that not all was lost. She could still reach for the stars, even from a wheelchair.

Finally the time came for her to go home and I knew, from personal experience, that it was going to be the toughest time of all. Judy must have sensed the same. She decided to organise a surprise for Maria. She and her friends asked if they could fly Jenny and me over to meet Maria, and speak at a fundraiser to help pay for modifications to her home. I couldn't get over there fast enough.

I'll never forget wheeling into Maria's friend's house. 'Gee, it's a bloody long way over here, Maria,' I said. She nearly fell out of her chair. Finally, we met face to face.

Experiences like these made me realise I could help others by telling my story. Perhaps I could impart some enthusiasm and the feeling that all was not lost, and in doing so, I was lifting myself as well. I also discovered helping someone is one of the greatest things in the world you can do. The rewards are priceless. And it's particularly special when they're on a similar journey to one you've experienced. Just like one truck driver likes swapping yarns with another truckie, or a doctor with another doctor, a teacher with other teachers. Just as birds of a feather flock together, people with similar life experiences like to compare notes.

In January 2003 I crossed paths with one of the most inspiring people I've ever had the privilege to meet – Christopher Reeve. It was a pure stroke of luck. A friend of mine knew Gabbi Cusack, a former nanny to Dana and Christopher's son, Will, and one of the organisers of 'Still Flying High', a dinner held at Fox Studios to raise money for spinal research at which Christopher was the speaker and main attraction. He was also invited to be the keynote speaker at the then NSW Premier, Bob Carr's spinal cord conference, 'Making Connections'.

Thanks to Gabbi, I was invited to participate in a panel during the conference and a couple of days later got to spend twenty very precious minutes talking to Christopher. I remember wheeling down to our meeting place thinking, 'Shit, what am I going to say. He's Superman and I'm just a farmer from Croppa Creek. What could he possibly find interesting or inspiring about me after what he's done?' I thought about what I'd read in the book he wrote, about his incredible attitude towards his injury, his starring roles in the Superman movies, how he was a huge Hollywood star and mates with other big names like Robin Williams. The list of his accomplishments went on and on. There were moments when I nearly could have turned around but I decided, 'You're on your way now, too late.'

He was already at the restaurant when we arrived, with his wife, Dana – who is one incredible lady – and son, Will. Gabbi organised a space for me right beside him. The first thing that I couldn't get over was how big he was, how powerful. Not only was Christopher Reeve naturally very tall, he'd also used electrical stimulation to retain his muscle tone, so he looked like this big athletic bloke sitting in a motorised wheelchair. Anyone with spinal cord injury can maintain their muscle tone like that, but it requires an enormous amount of time and effort and daily dedication. I've never bothered so my muscles have faded away to virtually nothing. They're all still there but because they don't work, they've shrunk.

Christopher had maintained his body in tiptop condition partly to ensure that if there was ever a breakthrough in medical research into repairing a spinal cord injury, he'd be ready to get back on his feet as soon as possible. He'd also been able to demonstrate that the body could recover extra function more than two years after the injury. He regained some movement in his fingers, wrists and certain other joints, and some sense of feeling throughout the rest of his body up to five years after falling from a horse and suffering a C2 spinal cord injury in 1995. What he also proved was that even movie stars, known across the world, could suffer a life-changing disability. Christopher inspired everyone with his amazing attitude. He was going to walk – full stop.

So there I was, meeting Christopher Reeve, nervous and overwhelmed as all hell. But within moments, he'd broken down the barrier. Immediately he was interested in my story, how I'd become a quadriplegic and what I did on the farm, about the bike and hoist and ultralight. He wanted to know how long I was staying in Sydney and when we were going home. He was so easy to talk to.

He told me how much he loved Australia and how he wanted to come back and next time see more of the countryside as well. I chatted on in a bubble of euphoria, oblivious to all else – this man beside me like a magnet, pulling me towards him with his power and aura. The memory of his attitude and energy will always be with me, as will an appreciation of the passion with which he fought for what he believed in and his dedication to fundraising for spinal cord research.

I met him again at Government House during a civic reception. He was in the line up of formal guests. Straightaway he recognised me.

'Hello, Sam.'

'Gidday, Christopher.'

'I've been thinking about some of the things that you do and I think it's just incredible.'

I couldn't believe he remembered me after all the people he'd met in Australia. He mentioned the ultralight and the farm. He'd remembered it all. When he left I thought, 'We could easily strike up a long-term friendship.'

But that wasn't to be. In October 2004 Christopher Reeve died. He was only fifty-two. I was devastated. So were a lot of people around the world. His death took away a powerful symbol of hope and inspiration for everybody, not just the disabled people of the world but the able-bodied too. It was like experiencing a campfire going out on a cold night in the outback then feeling the chill close in around you. Such a sense of loss, as the light disappears and your eyes slowly adjust to the darkness. But if you look up, you can always see the stars. In the same way the stars remain, my time with Christopher will never leave me.

I love public speaking. It's not only because it's rewarding to tell my story in the hope it might help others. It has also allowed me to meet lots of great people. I've met celebrities, like Christopher

Reeve, who I thought were on another level until I got to know them and realised they were just a father or a mother, a son or daughter, like everyone else. They all have thrills and spills in their lives too. But then there's the ordinary, everyday people I meet who are doing extraordinary things, like restoring farmland damaged by salinity, running outstanding nursing homes, developing leading stockfeed businesses, or dealing with illnesses or injuries of their own. They're not looking for rewards or accolades. They don't want gold medals. They're simply getting on with chasing their dreams.

When you get out and about, there are so many people in this country doing the most amazing things. Some are doing it under enormously difficult circumstances, but they don't mention it because that's just the way it is.

In an almost eerie coincidence, a few of the people I've met or known have also appeared on *Australian Story*. One was Dr Charlie Teo. I shook his hand for the first time literally in front of Christopher Reeve. Four months later he appeared on *Australian Story* in a program called 'The Trouble with Charlie'. Here was this down-to-earth, motorbike-riding bloke who turned out to be one of the country's top neurosurgeons, someone with an enormous talent.

Another was Matt Laffan, who appeared on *Australian Story* in April 2001 in a story called 'A Sense of Destiny'. He's a Sydney lawyer with diastrophic dysplasia. Within moments of meeting Matt, you forget about his electric chair or that his limbs haven't grown properly. You don't see his disability, you just see this wonderful bloke who immediately captivates people. His story inspired me so much I rang him. Straightaway we hit it off. We got onto rugby. His dad had coached NSW, mine had played for the

Wallabies and Matt was on the rugby judiciary. We found an instant connection and have kept in touch. Finally we met when we spoke together at the spinal cord conference in 2003. It's amazing how paths crisscross your life.

I saw Victoria Friend's *Australian Story* 'On the Mountain' in May 2003 – I'd known her during our school days – and Gayle Shann's story 'With this Ring' in April the same year. Believe it or not, her husband's grandmother lived on the property next door to Dick and Wapp at Longreach, where I worked the year after I left school. Both their stories blew me away and I rang each of these women to congratulate them on finding the courage to tell them. It was an incredibly difficult task for Victoria, as she had to deal with the heart-wrenching loss of the man she loved as she recovered from massive injuries suffered in the plane crash that killed him. The good news is that in 2005 she and Dermott Shannon, who also featured in her story, married and earlier this year they were expecting their first child.

Gayle also coped with horrific injuries. Her right arm was ripped off and her other paralysed in an accident with a posthole digger. She'd only been married three years. I was so gripped by her story and the dedication of her husband. What a fantastic bloke. If anyone saw that story and walked away without being moved, they must have been made of steel.

Then the *Australian Story* crew got wind of the fact a few of us were chatting behind their backs and decided they'd better do a story to expose it. 'Small World' went to air in June 2004. Again there was a terrific response.

It was followed by the *Australian Story* Roadshow in Brisbane during August of that year. It was an evening where the public could meet some of the people who'd featured on the program, and find out what had happened in their lives since their stories were broadcast. Again we met other people who had been on *Australian Story*, including the Victorian bootmaker-turned-opera-singer, Peter Brocklehurst; former national representative swimmer, Tracy Wickham; the police trying to solve the case of the disappearance of Sunshine Coast teenager Daniel Morcombe; and Dr Michael Holt, the Brisbane orthopaedic surgeon hit by a car, suffering head and face injuries. I returned home wanting to fly to the moon. If I'd come back and built a rocket to the moon every time I was inspired to do so, I wouldn't have a shed big enough to put all my rockets in. That's what *Australian Story* and the speaking has given me.

The other thing about friendships is the way they sometimes lead you in new, exciting directions. In September 2004 I was speaking in northeast Victoria and the organiser of my trip just happened to be great mates with Tom O'Toole. He organised for us to meet. Tom is one of the nation's most successful motivational presenters and owner of the Beechworth Bakery, which turns over millions of dollars worth of food annually. He wrote his story in a book called *Breadwinner*. I found Tom was totally down-to-earth and a bit rough around the edges, like me. He was also incredibly inspiring. He encouraged me to seriously consider pursuing public speaking as a profession.

A couple of months later fate stepped in again. I received an email from Zoe Vaughan from Claxton Speakers International in Sydney. She wrote, 'Having read your story, I was wondering if you have considered public speaking. It is not for everyone (some fear public speaking more than death) and I appreciate that you have a farm to run ... if you alone or yourself and Jenny together are interested, we would welcome the opportunity to speak with you in more detail about the industry.' Immediately I looked up Claxton's web page on the internet and there were all these superstars. I read their stories and what they'd done and thought, 'Jesus Christ ... why would they want me?'

In January 2005 Jenny and I met Zoe and the owner, Deb Claxton. We liked them instantly. Later we met Deb's husband, Phil, who was also a partner in the business and had grown up in Tamworth. We felt at home with him straightaway as well. We agreed to join Claxtons.

I'm very much a one-on-one kind of person. I'd rather pick up the phone than write an email. That might have something to do with the fact I'm a particularly slow one-finger typist. But it's also the way I like to do things. I prefer to speak to people and get to know them. In a sense Claxton Speakers International suits Jenny and me because it isn't the biggest speaking bureau in Australia – although it's growing rapidly – and the staff have made us feel welcome to what is still very much a new industry for us. So it's terrific to make that connection and we're now doing more speaking. We're still on the bottom rung of the ladder, but I can see a future ahead.

But what about the farm? Did I want to shut that gate? At this stage, the answer to that is no. I still love nothing more than to jump on the bike and chase a few cattle and feel the wind on my face. I like to think it's possible to have the best of both worlds. Time will tell.

The more speaking I've done, the more people who have told me I should write down my story. And with a wife who's a journalist, it seemed a natural progression. In fact, Jenny has been keen to write my book from the time we married. The *Women's Weekly* article, published the year of our wedding, mentioned that. In response, we had a note from a book agent called Selwa Anthony. We'd never heard of her, but she wrote us a great note saying if we ever decided to write a book she'd be interested in hearing from us. We filed it away and got busy doing other things.

In fact, during 2003 we put most of our efforts into trying to have a baby. Obviously it wasn't going to happen naturally, so we decided to try IVF. While everything appeared to go smoothly, it was an emotional battlefield as we waited to see if each step in the process would be successful. You don't realise how lucky you are if you can have children naturally, because a lot of things have to fall into place for it to happen and you're totally unaware of all that when nature takes its course.

Unfortunately for us, it wasn't successful. We then had to choose whether to keep trying or give up on that rainbow and go chase another one. It was a tough decision. We felt like we were letting down our parents, who would have loved to see us have children, and there also seemed to be a lot of social pressure to have kids. We agonised over the decision for months. But in the end we knew if we didn't have children it would give us the freedom to pursue other things, like the speaking and the book.

Once again, the book idea gained momentum. We finally decided to do something about it. So I rang Selwa. 'Sam Bailey, where have you been?' was her reaction. 'Why haven't you contacted me?' I might have needed persuading that the book was a goer, but she certainly didn't. She told us to write a synopsis and couple of chapters and send it to her as soon as we could. Again the time slipped away.

Then in 2004, Jenny noticed Selwa was speaking at the NSW Writers' Centre's Popular Fiction Festival – and we went down to Sydney to hear her speak. It was then that we realised how popular Selwa was. She is one of Australia's most sought-after book agents – particularly for aspiring popular fiction writers – and has launched the careers of many of the country's top authors. I realised at that festival there were heaps of people wanting to write books. Getting them published was a whole different ball game. Anyone can sit down and write a story, but it's pretty tough out there in the publishing world. Selwa mentioned she'd take questions after her talk and I found myself sitting in that crowded room – more than a hundred people attended the session – thinking, 'What am I going to do to win her over?'

While we'd already had contact with Selwa, I sensed I needed to cement that commitment. So she finished speaking and took some questions. I waited until the very last minute, then put up my hand.

'We've decided to write our story and I'm looking for a book agent. And I think you're really, really good-looking, so will you represent me?' Everyone cracked up.

Selwa jumped down from the stage and gave me a hug and kiss and said, 'Sam, send me something, please!'

So many people came up to me afterwards and said, 'Wish we'd thought of that.'

Eventually, with quite a lot of persuasion from Selwa and *Australian Story* presenter and author Caroline Jones, ABC Books agreed to give us a contract. It's a tremendous privilege. I know some people try forever to get a publisher and many eventually self-publish, while others throw their manuscripts in the bin in despair. I guess all I can say is never give up and don't be afraid to be different. It's always worked for me.

FOURTEEN

MY MATE QUADRIPLEGIA

There was a period in my life when I looked up to the heavens and said, 'Thanks very much,' expressing anger and resentment and despair that I'd become a quadriplegic. I thought the injury had taken away everything. It had taken away my dreams, my whole world as I knew it. It picked me up out of the world I was in and dropped me into a new and foreign place, where all the rules had changed. At the time, it was the biggest asshole of an experience. I felt I'd been pushed off a hillside and I hadn't just rolled, I'd dropped off a cliff. Welcome to my new mate quadriplegia.

But these days, nineteen years on, I look up and say, 'Thanks so much.' I now believe someone up there was bringing down on me good fortune, not bad, that day a car accident changed the path of my life forever. It has given me so much.

It's given me a whole new perspective on life. Now I appreciate what I had and what most people take for granted.

Mobility. I often sit in the car in the street while Jenny's shopping and watch someone hop out of their vehicle, shut the door, jump up on the footpath and walk off. I see a person approach a set of stairs and walk up without even looking, and then someone else run down. If only those people knew what it's like not to be able to do that. What they take for granted every day of their lives.

It makes me value what I've got left. The fact I can still use my arms and hands. They don't work properly but they do a lot of things. They still allow me to live reasonably independently, to be able to pick up a power tool and strip a piece of furniture, to fix a puncture in my motorbike tyre and most importantly, to wrap my arms around my little mate Jenny. That's the thing I appreciate most.

Quadriplegia has also given me a whole new set of values.

Most importantly, it's taught me patience – something seriously lacking before. It was hardly surprising. I was a six-foot-tall masculine, practical country bloke who could move mountains. I wasn't going to hang around waiting for someone to give me a hand. I could do everything myself – or so I thought. Today the simplest task, like hooking the slasher on the front of my motorbike, which would have once taken me a few seconds, now takes ages. Like a lot of things. In the beginning that wasn't easy to swallow but now I've learnt to accept that when you're a quadriplegic, things take time.

I also discovered I could accept a life-changing disability. No one knows until they face it. You can try to imagine what it would be like to be blind or deaf or have only one leg. You can shut your eyes or put your fingers in your ears or hop into a wheelchair, but you know it's not real. You never really know if you have that inner strength to get through and come out the other side of a serious injury or illness until you've experienced it. I have. And I've come out the other side, for which I'm eternally grateful.

Along the way I've acquired some fantastic mates, too. There are those who've been with me since my childhood or school or jackarooing days, whose friendships were strengthened by my accident. Some have asked me to be in their bridal parties. What a huge call. It means a wheelchair in their wedding photos and the hassles of making sure I'm not too hot or too cold, the bother of getting access for me into the church. Despite that, many have paid me the ultimate compliment. It makes me feel so humble.

Another thing I truly value is that I'm surrounded by a community of mammoth proportions. It's not big in size, but in each case their hearts are bigger than Phar Lap's. They've supported me and my family through thick and thin, looked out for me and cheered me at every milestone along the way. They'll pull over to check on me if I'm stopped along the roadway, just in case I need a hand, and share a joke and beer at every opportunity. If you could bottle it – the spirit of rural Australia – it would be worth a fortune. Warialda, Croppa Creek and their surrounds have it in bucketfuls. These are the people who've been with me through the whole journey. And they're the people I'll no doubt grow old with, long after I've been forgotten on the speaking circuit. I couldn't have done what I've done without them.

Then there are my new friends. As I've started to travel around the country, many people have inspired me with their own stories of hardship and grit and determination. Those ordinary, everyday people who are leading extraordinary lives. Who are fighting their own battles and winning, and making Australia what it is today. I value them too.

I've been very, very lucky along my journey because so many great people have come into my life and many have helped me along the way. I hope I've given them something too.

My life sounds wonderful, and it is, but I want you to know it's not all beer and skittles. There are days when I wonder why in the hell I ever got out of bed. When the wheels just fall right off. Everything goes pear-shaped.

Recently I had a day like that. It started with a phone call from a truckie I'd been waiting for. He'd had a breakdown and wouldn't be able to pick up grain at 6am. That immediately stuffed up my well-laid plans and I sensed instantly that it was going to be one of those days. If the truck wasn't loaded first thing, then the two blokes I'd organised to help him wouldn't be ready for the header mechanic later that morning. And so the day went on, nothing going according to plan or falling into place. All this took place on a 36-degree day and I was boiling – constantly having to douse myself with water to keep my temperature down. And then as if things weren't already bad enough, by afternoon wild storms were brewing on the horizon. One swept in so quickly it caught us unawares. I sent men madly tarping field bins and racing to put trucks under cover. And then the heavens opened up, bringing the harvest to a grinding halt. All in all, it was a shit of a day. You get that sometimes.

There was a time when I might have got seriously pissed off at the truckie, ranting and raving and shouting. But now I can see it didn't help and it certainly didn't solve the problem. In fact, it only made things worse.

Instead, I've learnt to jump the fence, so to speak. In my mind I jump over into someone else's paddock and just for ten seconds

I think about all the people in the world who don't have enough food to eat or lack something as simplistic as clean drinking water. I think about people who've had their whole lives gutted by war, terrorism or natural disasters. They'd all swap places with you in the blink of an eye.

Okay, so you think that's a bit far away? You can't relate to that? Then bring it closer to home. I think about the people who have lost loved ones in tragic accidents, people dying of terminal illnesses, or patients in oncology wards, spinal units or rehab units right around the country. You wouldn't swap places with them, would you?

Then pretty quickly I jump back over the fence into my paddock and it doesn't look so bad after all. My problems become insignificant. All I've got to worry about is a broken-down truck, no one to help the header mechanic and a bit of wild weather disrupting harvest. Okay, I can find another truck, delay the header mechanic and get the crop off later. And sure, it might be weather-damaged, but meanwhile there'll be plenty of feed for the cattle. So that's how I cope.

I also remember that you need to have a few bad days to properly appreciate the good ones. Tomorrow's another day and it will be better. My other coping mechanism is laughter. I've learnt to laugh things off, make a joke. Then I give Jenny a kiss, the dog a scratch and everything is okay.

Some people struggle with bad days. Occasionally, I meet individuals who are down and can't see any hope. It saddens me to see people like that. They've been crash-tackled by some sort of misfortune in their life but they haven't been able to get back up on their feet.

As far as I can see, there's no right or wrong in getting over tragedy. Some people grieve a lot longer than others. Some people accept loss a lot quicker than others. It depends on the individual and their situation. I was lucky because I was able to stand up, pick up the ball and keep running virtually straightaway.

And now I take further inspiration from the hope that I might be able to help others. Maybe I can make them stop and think, 'If Sam can get on with it so can I.' I want to make people glad they can stand up, walk out of the room and hop into a car. I want them to be thankful they've got family and friends and learn to appreciate them more. I want them to feel lucky they can watch the sun come up in the morning and appreciate living in this great country which offers so much opportunity to everyone, if they want to chase their dreams. I want them to focus on the positives, not the negatives.

I want them to focus on the future and not dwell on the past. Focus on what they want and most importantly, on what they have, because take it from me, if you can do that, life will be the most fabulous, the most amazing, the most incredible journey you're ever on.

The group I most enjoy trying to inspire to chase their dreams is young people. Each year I'm part of the Rotary Youth Leadership Awards (RYLA) program in southeast Queensland/ northeast NSW. It's fantastic. It helps a lot of troubled kids, some who are on drugs, have suffered sexual abuse, or have shattering family lives. Every time I leave there, I hope I might have sown a seed. It may take a week, it may take a month, it may take a year before it germinates — but maybe one day the seed will grow into something big.

Maybe I love speaking to kids because I'm still a kid at heart or maybe it's because they're still such an open book with endless possibilities. And perhaps it's because the more I travel and speak, particularly in schools, the more I see the need for someone to say, 'Come on, get on with it. You don't know how lucky you are to live in Australia.'

One thing I've discovered is the chasm between primary school and secondary school children. Primary kids are so innocent and open. They want to know what happens when you get bogged in your wheelchair and how heavy your leg is to lift and they want to see you do a burnout on the floor. They have endless questions. And then inevitably, they start telling you all their own stories – how Grandfather broke his ankle, and how their puppy got its head caught in a tin and died. Their enthusiasm is so alive and undamaged. I feel I can make an enormous difference at that age. And there's the extra message they take from me about road safety. I'm living, breathing evidence of what can happen if you don't wear a seat belt.

Secondary kids are completely different. They're more reserved and reluctant to ask questions in a classroom. It's scarily easy for them to be derailed. There's so much pressure on them from their peers, parents and society. At a time when they should be just being kids, they're choosing subjects that can affect the whole direction of their lives. Some are trying to deal with broken families, problems at home and challenges of their own. A burden like that combined with enormous peer pressure can amount to a lethal cocktail.

Again with teenagers, I simply sit and tell my story and I get straight to the point. I tell them the good, the bad and the ugly.

Of course, they don't ask many questions because they're terrified the other kids will think they're uncool or a dag or something. They prefer to talk to you one on one.

Sometimes the best way to start them talking is to ask them about themselves. I asked one quite attractive girl in a high school in Victoria what she was going to do when she finished school. She folded her arms and said, 'I'm going to be a bum.' I thought how sad this was. Here was this nice-looking girl, able-bodied, with her whole life ahead of her, but her body was slumped, negativity affecting the whole way she held herself.

'You don't really want to be a bum, do you?' Jenny asked her later.

'No ...'

'What do you really want to do?'

'I dunno ... I'll probably end up being a hairdresser or something,' she said. 'There's something else I'd really like to do but there's no point telling you about that because I can't do it anyway.'

'What is it?'

'There's no point telling you ... I'll never be able to do it.'

Jenny finally convinced her to reveal her real dream. It turned out she wanted to work in the music industry, managing bands. What a great job, and what an original thing to want to do.

Later Jenny and I discussed that conversation. Jenny said, 'From the time I was fifteen I knew exactly what I wanted to be – a journalist. I know now how lucky I was. Like Sam, I had my dream and was going to pursue it no matter how long and hard I had to work to get it. Because I had in my head what I wanted and believed it would happen – maybe not tomorrow or the next day, but one day – it came true. And the amazing thing is, when you have that dream clear in your mind, it often comes to you sooner rather than later. I had a cadetship on a country newspaper within three months of leaving school. But I had done everything I could to chase that dream, and kept going despite many rejections. Throughout my career, every time I didn't get a job, I rang up and asked why. And then I'd make sure the same thing didn't hold me back next time. You don't have to be dux of your class to achieve your dreams – you've just got to believe it can happen.'

We like to think we might have sown a seed at the high school in Victoria that day. We'll never know of course, but we hope we might have put a tiny chink in that girl's armour. Perhaps we had enough impact to stop her ending up on the streets or on drugs, and maybe, just maybe, she's chasing her dreams. I hope so.

I love public speaking. It's fantastic to travel, to be away sometimes and meet all these great people, but it's also exhausting. Sometimes I forget I am a quadriplegic. I find it tiring being in airports and a bit stressful, not always knowing where we're going. It's nice visiting a city and staying in ritzy motels for a couple of days, but shit it's good to return home and look at the stars and be able to pat the dog. It's great to get on my bike and ride around the cattle.

One of the things I love about coming home to the farm is the way it brings me back to earth. One day we might be eating oysters at Darling Harbour, the next we can be in the cattle yards, in the dust and flies and covered in shit. It's a real leveller and reminds me that, at the end of the day, I'm just a busted-ass farmer from the middle of nowhere.

There's one particular time when I was really brought back down to earth with a thud, or I should say splat. Jenny and I were wandering through the cattle pavilion at the Sydney Royal Easter Show. It was 1998 – the first time it had been held at the new showground at Homebush.

Jenny was working on the *Country Hour* so I deliberately waited until she was finished work to look at the show cattle, knowing she'd want to see them too. We spent ages wandering down all the aisles, looking at the livestock and chatting with friends. Everyone was struck with how spotless it all was in this lovely new pavilion that had been purpose-built. It was state-of-the-art and had pathways that were great for me in my chair. And of course, the cattle were all fed up to the eyeballs with grain and various sorts of feed to bring them up to their best for the show. They stood in rows, glowing coats and fat rear-ends displayed for all to see.

An hour or so later we were making our way out, walking down the last row of cattle in the quiet end of the pavilion – literally fifteen metres from the doorway. We were moving along quickly now; nobody was about and only a handful of cattle remained. Suddenly a bovine cough broke the quiet in this lonely, out-of-the-way corner of the pavilion. And as the heifer coughed, she lifted her tail and a projectile of warm, runny green slime exploded across the aisle. I happened to be right in the firing line. It sprayed all over my collar and tie, splattered across my shoulder and even the mobile phone in my shirt pocket. It hung from the spokes of the wheels of my chair. It was not a pretty sight. The only part of me that escaped the deluge was my head.

I couldn't believe what had happened. There I was at the Royal Easter Show, dressed in my best shirt and tie, and I'd just been sprayed in smelly, runny manure. I thought, 'It's not real. I'm dreaming. Any moment, my life will rewind and it won't have happened at all because it couldn't be possible.'

But the seconds passed, and the sticky, wet deposit didn't disappear. Slowly, reality sunk in. Here I was, far from bathrooms and clean clothes and I really was, quite literally, covered in shit. It was incomprehensible. I didn't know what to say or do.

Meanwhile Jenny wasn't any help at all. She was laughing so hard she was doubled over with cramps. Tears poured down her face. 'Terrific,' I thought. 'Here's the girl I'm going to spend the rest of my life with, this thing has happened and she thinks it's hilarious, one of the funniest things she's ever seen.' Not that Jenny had escaped unscathed. Warm, wet manure dripped down the side of her dress, from her thigh down, but I had copped the full force.

Further up the aisle two young blokes were looking after some cattle. We wheeled up and told them what happened. They no doubt thought it was hilarious but weren't quite game to laugh. They didn't know what to suggest. They only had cleaning materials they'd used on their cattle – buckets, sponges and old towels.

We decided that would have to do. So Jenny sponged me down as best she could, shook the mobile phone, and removed as much of the manure from the spokes of the chair as possible. She did a reasonable job. Although she got rid of the bulk of the residue, it left behind these brown/green stains on my chambray shirt – and the smell. I smelt like I'd rolled in a cattle feedlot. It wafted like aftershave.

Then I faced the crowds. Actually, the response was hilarious, an interesting study in human nature. Nobody said a word. Obviously they didn't dare. They were too polite. But once we told a few people what had happened, it was like taking the brakes off an express train. They laughed their heads off. And they admitted they'd been wondering about the stains all over my shirt and tie. Despite the mishap, we stayed at the show for a while. I doused my sorrows with plenty of beers and that helped a little. But then there was the trip back to Central station. We did try to explain to people on the train what had happened and why I smelt so bad, but they were city people and thought we were quite crazy, I'm sure.

It was another example of events in my life coinciding to make something happen. A split second either side of that heifer's rear end, I would have been all right. And I could sit behind the same heifer for a million years and it wouldn't happen again. Like my appointment with quadriplegia way back in 1987, some things are just meant to be.

Do I ever imagine a day when I don't have the farm in my life? Maybe. But at this stage Jenny and I enjoy the best of both worlds. Perhaps this is the beginning of the end; maybe the gate is slowly closing on my farming life. I can't imagine it closing completely, but you never know. Maybe I've been there, done that. After all, I've been helping on the farm now for almost nineteen years. Possibly I've achieved as much as I can. It's been immensely rewarding, but I know I can't go on slogging my body forever.

Maybe it's fate. I've been presented with this other opportunity so I can take it easier on my body. It might be better for Jenny and less stressful all round. Maybe there's someone up there directing traffic. I'm certain the path will become clear as time progresses.

Sometimes you've got to walk out on a plank. You might get halfway and decide you want to go back, then again you might want to dive off the end. It's like anything, you have to give it a try. But don't be disappointed if it doesn't work. Life's like that – sometimes it's not for you. Don't give up, though. If you can't chase that rainbow, go and chase another one. It may be that you need to go halfway along the plank to get onto the next one, or you'll meet someone who knows someone else who gives you a phone number, and it leads you down the path you're meant to be on.

The longer my life goes on, the more certain I am that I'm meant to be in a wheelchair. Why else would I have been given so many blessings that so perfectly fit and enhance my life as a quadriplegic?

For one thing, I seem to have incredibly long arms. It seems funny, doesn't it? I seem to be able to reach things easily. I can reach up onto quite a high shelf or down onto the ground. I can stretch to start a pump. Reach is terribly important when you're in a wheelchair. My skin also seems to be surprisingly tough. I've never had a pressure sore and when I take off skin, it heals very quickly, although at times I do spend days, even weeks, in bed recovering from minor injuries.

It's striking how my body seems to be able to cope with the rough and tumble of farming and the way things have come into my life to make it all possible. The fact that I saw a hoist in the back of that ute in Moree or that my closest town had an ultralight club or that I said 'no' to a radio interview over the phone that day. They're all things that confirm my belief it was part of the plan.

And Jenny is sure she was meant to share my journey. She said, 'I believe our life's path is predestined from the very beginning. I know many people would argue about that, but I sense things happen for a reason. Perhaps it's only my way of justifying events that take place in my life – a delusory ploy to cushion the ups and downs of life. All the same, that's how I feel. And meeting Sam has only cemented that view because I feel as though I've been preparing to be his partner for most of my life.

'Perhaps Sam didn't wear his seatbelt on that fateful day back in 1987 so he could bring hope to other people and perhaps I became a journalist so I could help him tell his story. Until I was fifteen I wasn't going to be a journalist. I really wanted to be a jillaroo or polo groom. But then I went to the local newspaper for work experience – more on a whim than a passion – and from the very first day I loved it. I knew I'd found the thing I most wanted to do with my life.' Maybe Jenny was being prepared to write these very words.

My former TAS house master, Jim Graham, had a wonderful perspective on my view that I was meant to be in a wheelchair. He was heavily involved in the production of plays at the school, and many years ago he helped stage one outdoors. It worked very well and they decided to do it annually. As the director, he figured that if they were going to all the trouble of putting it on outside in the elements, with the extra cost and effort of outdoor seating, discomfort to the audience and risk of weather, it had to be done in such a way that people thought it belonged outside.

He said, 'It could not be an inside play, transported outdoors. We had to do it in a way that gave it its own integrity, otherwise why in the hell do it outside? In my own eyes it could not be really successful unless, when it was over, people went away saying, "How the hell could they do that play inside?", "How could it have been any other way?"'

To him, it was not a question of whether I was 'meant' to be in a chair before my accident but rather what came after. It was about how I lived my life as a quadriplegic, and how that made it impossible to imagine being any other way. It was about making it work, so it appeared that it was meant to be and I belonged there. I'm not sure if he's right or I am – which comes first, the chicken or the egg? But I know I wouldn't have my life any other way.

People sometimes ask me if researchers find a way to connect my spinal cord back up again, would I do it?

No, I wouldn't. I know what I've put my body through in the last nineteen years. I've heard cracks and creaks and groans that let me know, if I could feel, I would have experienced plenty of pain. And it goes on still. Only the other day I was chasing some cattle, my foot fell off the footplate and was whacking against the ground. If I could feel the aftermath of all my injuries and almost two decades of wear and tear I might be in a huge amount of pain. After all, human shoulders aren't designed to constantly lift eighty kilos day in, day out.

Plus I've been in a wheelchair for such an enormous length of time that I think it would take a huge amount of physiotherapy to get me up and moving. And at the end of the day, what am I achieving that I haven't got now? Just mobility really. That's the main thing I miss.

But if the day came when they could hook me back up and I could see that twelve months of physio might get me back some mobility, maybe my bowel and bladder might operate a bit more easily, and I might cope with extremes of temperature better, I might consider it. If I could see it really would make my life a little easier. But I think I'm so far down the track now that I'd probably rather stay the way I am.

Nevertheless I desperately hope they do find a cure because there is a lot of hurt, sadness and loss caused by spinal cord injury. As I've already mentioned, I'm sure people will arrive in hospital one day with a severed spinal cord, be connected up and a few weeks later they'll walk out. It's only a matter of time.

Meanwhile I want to get on with my life rather than spend my time and energy trying to walk again. I'm not critical of people who focus on walking. If that's their wish, I'm right behind them. But I would say, 'While you're doing all that, is your life passing you by? And if they don't find a cure for another twenty years – which I certainly hope doesn't happen – how will you feel then? Will you have wasted a lot of your life in the meantime?' There's no right or wrong, but I reckon you should enjoy today. Fulfil your dreams now.

If someone said to me, 'We'll return you to 1987 and give you your legs back.' Would I do it? We'll take away the accident and the spinal injury, make you six foot tall and bullet-proof again. Would I want it? We'll take you back and make you walk again. Would I prefer it?

No. No. No.

There's no way I'd go back and start again. If I did, I'd miss out on all the things I've had in the past nineteen years. I might never have gone snow skiing or travelled overseas or flown an ultralight. I might not have learnt to value the love and strength of my family – Mum, Dad, Bill and Kate – and all my extended family. I might not have found out just how fantastic and supportive some of my friends could be. I certainly wouldn't have lived a life that inspired the interest of a journalist and gave me the chance to find my soulmate, Jenny.

I would never have become friends with one of the oldest living quadriplegics in Australia, Mike Warden. I wouldn't have spent twenty amazing minutes with Christopher Reeve and met people like Charlie Teo and Matt Laffan. I wouldn't have been on *Australian Story* and got to know Deb Fleming and Caroline Jones. I wouldn't be travelling the country telling my story and working with Claxtons. I wouldn't have had a note from Selwa Anthony and got to write this book. And most important of all, I would never have known I had the inner strength to face up to my mate quadriplegia. Because without him, none of this would have been possible.

ACKNOWLEDGEMENTS

Thank you to ABC Books for allowing me to tell my story, especially Stuart Neal, who believed in it enough to allow it to happen, with lots of encouragement from *Australian Story*'s Caroline Jones and my book agent Selwa Anthony. Thanks to ABC Books managing editor Brigitta Doyle, editor Jacquie Kent, and copy editor Anne Reilly, who all helped make it a better book thanks also to publicist Jane Finemore and Alan Davidson.

Thanks to many others, including my spinal unit doctor Bill Davies, nurse Libby Urquhart, who remembers better than me the night I almost died, her sister Dr Sue Urquhart, for her medical advice, ABC Television's *Australian Story* executive producer Deb Fleming, producer Caitlin Shea, cameraman Anthony Sines and editor Roger Carter; for their memories of filming my story and continuing friendship.

Thanks to my mentor Mike Warden and his wife Marg, for their inspirational love story and involvement in my own romance, Jim Graham for his guiding hand in my youth, and John Ryan for a wonderful friendship through thick and thin, and all their memories of those times.

Thanks also to Bruce McMullen, who taught me to fly and climb my own personal Mount Kosciusko, Richard Browning for his recollections of those early months in the spinal unit, and other friends and family who have helped to fill in the gaps with their stories. This book would not have been complete without them.

Special thanks must go to my parents, Graham and Libby Bailey, brother Bill and sister Kate, for their support, love and strength during my rollercoaster life – despite the fact their lives were irrevocably changed as a result of my accident. They also gave their memories freely.

And finally, none of this would have come to fruition if it hadn't been for the love-of-my-life and best mate Jenny, who spent months researching, interviewing, transcribing and writing this book. It never would have happened if it hadn't been for her encouragement and belief that my story should be told.